Flying Squirrels as Pets

Flying Squirrels as Pets. Facts and Information.

Including Japanese, Northern and Southern
Flying Squirrels.

Habitat, diet, adaptations, health, care and where
to buy all included.

by

by Elliot Lang

Published by IMB Publishing 2013

Introduction

Flying squirrels are just such lovely creatures, both in the wild and as pets. Growing to about ten inches, but able to leap twenty to thirty feet, these amazing undomesticated animals can make wonderful pets. With careful planning and a lot of hard work, they can be so rewarding to keep and very entertaining in their own right.

As with all exotic pets, flying squirrels have specific food and enrichment needs and require special care and attention in order to live happily and healthily in captivity. In order to keep flying squirrels as pets, you need to have a good understanding of their needs and any problems that could arise.

Flying squirrels can make wonderful pets to the right people and with the right preparation, flying squirrels can be very happy in captivity. They need lots of stimulation and enrichment as well as a lot of love and care. This book will look at everything you need to know when making your decision about whether or not to keep these sweet little creatures. It will go through all of their requirements and the possible pitfalls of keeping flying squirrels.

If you do decide you want a flying squirrel, this book can help you prepare for your new arrival, as preparation is the key. A flying squirrel is a real commitment, but if you choose to make that commitment, you can learn every thing you need to know and make a lasting, rewarding relationship. It is important to remember that flying squirrels are essentially wild animals. If you want your flying squirrel to be happy and healthy, you need to let them express natural behaviour. Being allowed to climb, chew and forage is vital to the emotional and physical health of the animal. As an owner it is your responsibility to make sure that your pet has access to everything it needs. This doesn't just mean food, water and shelter but the emotional and mental needs as well. The wellbeing of any animal in your care is your responsibility by law. This book aims to help you prepare for the arrival of your new flying squirrel.

Chapter 1. Flying squirrels

1. What exactly is a flying squirrel?

Flying squirrels are all from the family Pteromyini, and are basically very similar. Native to North America, Russia, Africa, Asia, China, Thailand and Japan, flying squirrels have been around longer than any other squirrel species alive today. Flying squirrels are rodents with a patagium, or membrane of skin, stretched between the forelimbs and hind limbs on each side, allowing them to 'fly'. Though the flying squirrel doesn't truly fly, they can glide quite gracefully for up to thirty feet. Though some sources claim they can glide for up to one hundred and fifty feet, this will rarely be seen in pet animals. This large skin flap is attached to the animal's body by a remarkably adapted cartilage rod, which you can see sticking out on the foreleg when they glide. When the patagium isn't in use, special muscles contract and pull it out of the way so that these wonderful little critters can scurry about unencumbered by the excess skin. They can be between 3 inches and 23 inches long depending on species. Flying squirrels commonly kept as pets in the west tend to be about an inch at birth (plus 1.5 inches worth of tail) and grow to about 10 inches including tail. The flying squirrel is a rodent of the family Sciuridae, which includes ground squirrels, flying squirrels, tree squirrels, chipmunks, marmots and prairie.

A flying squirrel is not the same as a sugar glider. Whilst they seem very similar, as they are both gliding arboreal omnivores that are most active at night, they are actually very different. Native to Australia, sugar gliders are from the possum family, as you can probably guess from their appearance. They are marsupials, meaning that, although they give birth to live young and suckle them, the young they give birth to are foetal at only 15 days of development, and continue to develop once they have attached themselves to their mothers teat, where they will remain for over 2 months.

2. General (types): the many faces of flying squirrels

There are 15 species of flying squirrel in the United States, split into to two main sub tribes. The flying squirrels kept as pets are from both of these tribes- Southern and Northern flying squirrels. As the names suggest, they are from, consecutively, the Southern and Northern states of North America. Here they have evolved into many different sub sets, often only having subtle differences.

In the United States you are more likely to find the indigenous species as pets than flying squirrels from elsewhere. Their food is native and easier to come by, they tend to be less affected by illnesses carried by local animals than those from elsewhere and their care, in terms of temperature etc, is simpler to deal with. The Southern and Northern flying species are then divided into sub species that differ only slightly, based on their location. The real differences are between the two tribes themselves, not between individual groups.

The southern flying squirrel is a little smaller and slightly sandier in colour than the northern flying squirrel. The northern flying squirrel has browner fur, which fades into a reddish brown along its back. The northern flying squirrel has a white tummy with the hairs fading to grey at their base, where the southern flying squirrel has tummy fur that is white all the way to the roots. One of the main differences between these two groups is breeding. The northern flying squirrel will have only one litter a year, where the southern flying squirrel will have 2 litters, one in early spring, the second in summer.

Their diets are roughly the same, but northern flying squirrels eat more coniferous foods - pine nuts and seeds - where the as the southern flying squirrel prefers the larger tree nuts available in hardwood forests. Both types of these flying squirrels eat nuts tree blossoms, fungi seeds, berries, fruits, insects, eggs and even the odd smaller rodent. But what makes the southern flying squirrel more successful in the wild is it's propensity for taller, older trees and it's ability to travel without unbroken forest. The larger northern flying squirrel is threatened in some parts, as it does not do so well in smaller patches of woodlands.

Captive care of these two species are identical. They need the same construction of enclosure of the same size. The only difference is that the southern flying squirrels may require more nuts in their diets that the northern, though this is one situation where your pet will guide you - just feed them what they seem to like best. They need the same level of care and attention as any type of flying squirrels and they can play the same games and enjoy the same toys and enrichments.

The real question when choosing a flying squirrel breed as a pet is the temperament. This is going to be the most important thing, as your flying squirrel could live for up to 15 years and you don't want to be lumbered with a pet that you don't get on with for this long. There is no real difference in temperament, though owners of each type argue that their chosen breed is the best.

There are 43 species of flying squirrel recognised around the world. They range from the tiny pygmy flying squirrel (Petaurillus kinlochii), found in Pakistan, weighing about 7oz; to the rare woolly flying squirrel (Eupetaurus cinereus), also found in Pakistan, that can weigh over 10 times as much.

Because of their evolutionary success, the flying squirrel can be found in various guises around the world. They have quite a range.

In Asia there are 8 types of giant squirrel, in the Petaurista genus. These are not generally kept as pets in the UK or US but they bond in the same way as the smaller ones that are kept in the west, but in parts of Russia and China they keep the larger, giant flying squirrels, that are available locally to them.

The Hodgson's giant flying squirrel (Petaurista magnificus) is found in the temperate forests of India and Nepal. This large, red and black flying squirrel is now classed as near to extinction due to habitat destruction.

The red giant flying squirrel (Petaurista petaurista) is fairly wide ranging. They can be found in Afghanistan, India, Pakistan, Kashmir, Java, Sri Lanka and Taiwan. These shorthaired red flying squirrels are much more successful than the Hodgson's as they migrate to find more food in conifer plantations.

The Chinese giant (yellow-eared) flying squirrel (Petaurista xanthotis) is a sleek, elegant creature with very dark fur, lined with black and red.

Chapter 1. Flying Squirrels

The red & white giant flying squirrel (Petaurista alborufus) is found in Thailand, Taiwan and is ridiculously cute! They're fluffy and ginger and blond and sweet, (not that I'm biased).
The spotted (lesser grey-headed) giant flying squirrel (Petaurista elegans) are found in China, Malaysia, Nepal, Myanmar, Vietnam, Indonesia and Laos. They don't just have grey heads but a wide grey band from their nose to their tail.

The Japanese giant flying squirrel (Petaurista leucogenys) from Japan looks more like a ground squirrel than any of the other flying squirrels do, as it is red with a cream tummy and a big, bushy tail.

South Indian giant flying squirrel (Petaurista philippensis) come from China, India, Myanmar and Sri Lanka.
Noble giant flying squirrel (Petaurista nobilis) from Bhutan is classed as near extinct.

The flying squirrels kept in the United States tend to be native ones, of the Genus Glaucomys. The Northern flying squirrel is beautiful and makes a wonderful pet. They have a cinnamon brown on the top and greyish colored sides with a white stripe down the centre of their tummies. Their eyes are big and round and their tail is flat and wide. They're about 25cm-37cm long and weigh between 115 grams and 240 grams. Southern flying squirrels are quite a bit smaller than the Northern flying squirrel and their whole underside is a creamy colour. Other than this they are fairly similar.

The smaller flying squirrels are the pygmies and the dwarfs. The most popular small squirrels as pets, mainly in the UK and Europe, are the Japanese dwarf flying squirrel (Pteromys momonga) and the Malaysian lesser pygmy flying squirrel (Petaurillus emiliae). These diminutive creatures are similar to their larger relatives in both their biology and their ability to bond closely with their humans. Not only this, but because of the small size of their bodies and heads in relation to their eyes (which are not much smaller than those of their American cousins) they always have a rather sweet look of surprise on their faces.

If you aren't going to go for a southern or a northern flying squirrel, you could look to eastern Europe and Asia. The main differences with flying squirrels from these parts of the world are the size. Here your choice of size can really vary, from the tiny lesser pygmy flying squirrel in Malaysia to the huge Woolly giant flying squirrel of Russia. Both of these species are endangered and they are not currently available to the pet trade. If you are looking for something very big or something very small, you could look to Japan. The dwarf and the giant flying squirrel are very similar to other flying squirrels.

Flying squirrels of all types make good pets, so your decision about which flyer to choose can mainly be based on what is available where you are. In the United States the choice is really between Southern and Northern but they are both very affectionate and there is no real difference in the sorts of health problems they face. In the United Kingdom the varieties kept may be more varied, but again, the types available will probably make your decision for you.

3. Flying squirrels in their natural environment

Wild Flying squirrels are opportunity feeding omnivores. They eat insects, fruit and seeds, but primarily they are granivorous mostly eating grain, seeds and nuts. They are the only truly nocturnal squirrels, in order to avoid daytime predators and competition for food. This is ideal for their foraging, as cockroaches and crickets are most active in the dark. Flying squirrels find food such as insects and seeds in the high branches of trees, which they occasionally munch on, as they love fruit, bark and sap. They also forage in the undergrowth and the rich, loamy leaf mould of the forest floor. Here they find insects, grubs, nuts and seeds, as well as sprouting vegetation and mushrooms.

Dwelling in forests across the world, the flying squirrel is perfectly evolved for arboreal living. They glide effortlessly from tree to tree, folding up their gliding flap, or patagium, out of the way while they dextrously clamber about on the ground or in the branches.

All flying squirrels are incredibly social and can live in groups of up to 8 in a nest. They nest in hollows in trees, often making use of abandoned woodpecker holes. Individuals of the same sex will often nest together in groups over winter for warmth and companionship. During the mating season they will find flying squirrels of the opposite sex and pair off.

As small prey animals, the flying squirrel has to be very careful and adaptive. Owls and hawks will take a flying squirrel easily, picking them off as a meal for themselves or for their young. Even a small bird of prey, say a 50oz hawk, can eat a whole flying squirrel per day and a large owl with chicks in the nest will happily take as many as she can catch.

Small mammals such as martens and weasels often prey on flying squirrels as they are so much smaller! A marten could happily eat 2 small flying squirrels a day.

Chapter 1. Flying Squirrels

Even hungry coyotes will sometimes eat a flying squirrel, though this would hardly satiate the hunger and a flying squirrel is hardly worth the effort for these larger predators.

Flying squirrels make it more difficult for their predators by their nocturnal habit, though this doesn't put off the owls!

As a result of these factors, most flying squirrels will only live for 4 years or so in the wild. This doesn't just effect flying squirrel populations, but also impacts on their environment. Flying squirrels are useful for spreading fungi spores all over their woodland territory. Some believe that flying squirrels in coniferous forests are useful for spreading the cones of conifers and pines, but others think this may be fallacious, as they do eat conifer and pine seeds.

When they are threatened they chirp quietly or click a warning. Flying squirrels communicate with each other by being affectionate. They rub each others faces with their own and release smells to express their emotions with pheromones and hormones, which are released from glands below the eye, as in other rodents.

Flying squirrels in the wild can cause all sorts of problems. The problem they've been known to cause is nesting in barns or houses inhabited by people or livestock. While a flying squirrel in the attic may sound like a cute little house mate, they can be a real nuisance, scurrying about keeping people awake at night and chewing on electrical cables.

Because of human integration in their environment, wild flying squirrels are increasingly coming into contact with humans and this can cause conflict.

Chapter 1. Flying Squirrels

Unfortunately, this reliance on forest habitat has caused 2 types of American flying squirrel, the North Carolina northern flying squirrel and the West Virginia northern flying squirrel, to become endangered. Flying squirrels, studies suggest, struggle to travel in non-forested areas. As their environment and natural domain shrinks to give way to human farming and living needs, these animals are squeezed out onto tiny remaining pockets of woodland where they are safe. In the late 1800's and early 1900's 500,000 acres of forest playing home to these two species, were reduced to a diminutive 200 acres, leaving many of them displaced, disorientated and homeless. A vast number died, meaning that in 1985, the North Carolina northern flying squirrel was listed as endangered. There are other types of flying squirrels that have become endangered across the world, though it tends to be the giant flying squirrels, as the declining forest cannot support their voracious appetites.

A wild flying squirrel can be a real nuisance to people wherever they are, in controlled forests, gardens or homes. It may seem odd, as they are native to forests and wooded areas, but flying squirrels can kill trees by ring barking them. This is where the bark and the under bark is removed in a continuous ring around the trunk, letting in infection and effectively starving the tree.

In gardens the problem is often more of an aesthetic one. They can strip plants of flowers, dig up bulbs and generally make a pest of themselves. This does not endear them to keen gardeners, park wardens or grounds keepers.

They get into roof spaces and scamper about at night making noises and disturbing peoples pets and people's sleep. Worse than this, though, is the damage they could be doing to the house while they're scampering about up there. They can denature the insulation, and, if they have a favorite place to pee in the eves, they can rot the wood away.

They chew power cables and water pipes causing all manner of havoc. The lead powder used to lubricate the casing over the cables is quite sweet and many wild flying squirrels that come into close contact with human settlements have learned this.

In winter 2011 a flying squirrel got trapped in the ER of a hospital in New Jersey. When fire fighters arrived to help it get out, the animal evaded capture for quite a while, by jumping at walls, climbing lamps and generally causing a commotion.

This incident didn't turn out to be very dangerous in the end, but if the flying squirrel in question had become entangled in any of the equipment it could have been injured of killed. If it had panicked and bitten a patient then it would have had to be put down and the patient could have contracted sepsis, typhus or another type of infection in the wound or the blood.

Wild flying squirrels can carry all sorts of ticks, parasites and flees that can pose a real health risk if in close proximity. Their droppings, if left and not cleared up properly, can cause a serious biohazard. Un treated fecal matter can grow mold, the spores of which can cause illness and can spread rapidly around the home.

Some wild flying squirrels can carry very unpleasant skin conditions that are caused by tiny insect lavas and which are communicable to humans, such as scabies and chiggers.

Chapter 2. Japanese Flying Squirrels

There are two very different types of flying squirrel in Japan. The Japanese Dwarf flying squirrel and the much larger Japanese Giant flying squirrel are so very different in many ways, but are both, very definitely, flying squirrels, as they both glide using their patagium and are both nocturnal, granivorous omnivores with a natural tendency towards calcium deficiency. They are also both rodents and genetically similar to flying squirrels all around the world. If you ignore the size, they are very similar to look at, both having a creamy white under side and a darker back for most of the year. They also have the big, round eyes that make them such appealing pets.

The main deference in colour is that in the winter the Japanese Dwarf will often, though not always, change colour. The sandy brown fur on the back of the animal will become much paler and they can turn an almost white shade of grey. The Japanese Dwarf flying squirrel is only a fraction of its much larger cousin, being only 20cm, just under 7in in length and weighing just 150g. The Japanese Giant flying squirrel, on the other hand, can grow up to 90cm or 34.5in and weigh as much as 1.5kg.

For flying squirrels this different, in size alone, you would need quite different enclosures, as the smaller Dwarf will be able to live in an enclosure much smaller than the larger Giant.

For the Japanese Dwarfs, you would need something with much closer spaced bars. Something like a chinchilla cage or a double deck rabbit enclosure would be ideal, as they still need to be able to glide about and climb.

Chapter 2. Japanese *Flying Squirrels*

The Japanese Giants would need something much bigger and you might even have to look at having something specially constructed. Due to their size, they are not quite so agile as some of the other flying squirrels, and their requirement for a larger cage isn't based purely on the physical space they take up, but on their need to be able to land safely. Owners of the Japanese Giant flying squirrel may argue differently, but they are no where near as graceful in confined spaces as smaller flying squirrels.

Other than that, the care is pretty similar, with them needing the same sorts of foods but in different quantities. They will eat about their body weight every 4 days, so the amount you feed them should be adjusted accordingly.

Chapter 3. Flying Squirrels as pets

1. History and original source of pet flying squirrels

Flying squirrels have been kept as pets since the early colonisation of America. The early settlers took cats and dogs and other domesticated pets, but soon the lure of the exotic and fascinating new animals overcame them, who could resist a little flying squirrel? Flying squirrels were amongst the most desirable of these 'wild' pets, as they were relatively easy to tame from a young age. In the 1700s other European colonists in the north of the country kept them as pets. When someone found out that flying squirrels would run on an exercise wheel, colonial blacksmiths began making cute little cages in the forms of mills with waterwheels.

There are paintings of young children with flying squirrels on little leads and they feature in early colonial art. In 1766 the famous American painter John Singleton Copley painted a portrait of his half brother, Henry, playing with his pet flying squirrel.

2. Is this the pet for you? pros and cons of flying squirrels

With a lifespan in captivity of up to 12 years, a flying squirrel is a real commitment. They need a lot of specialist treatment and handling - many owners handle their flying squirrels for upwards of six hours a day. They need more space than you would expect for an animal of their size. They should have occasional access to live food. When a flying squirrel gets ill you may struggle to find a vet who will know what to do or how to treat it. If you fail to bond with your flying squirrel you can find it very disappointing and disheartening. A young flying squirrel may need some hand rearing and this can be dangerous and may even kill your baby. They can become aggressive (though this is rare) during breeding season. If your flying squirrel gets a bit grumpy, you will have to keep handling it to stop it becoming completely anti-social, as it is bad for its mental well-being as well as yours as the pet owner.

The main reason for most pets to be given up, re housed or handed over to pet charities is a lack of knowledge. When making your decision about flying squirrels you need to ask yourself a couple of questions about both how prepared you are for a flying squirrel, and about whether or not you should get one, hard as it may be, you need to really think it through. The decision not to get a flying squirrel is just as important as the decision to get one and it does not reflect negatively on you if, once everything is considered, you decide you just don't have the time, emotional capacity or resources to be able to give your flying squirrel everything they need. It is a very important decision and you need to make sure everyone in your house is ready for the new arrival.

Important questions before you go any further:

Can you afford it? They can be very costly, not just in the initial outpay on the animal itself but the feeding and housing requirements also need to be taken into consideration. As well as this, you may need to pay out for medical expenses, (vet bills, medicine and travel to and from the vets if they're not close).

Will you be available to clean the enclosure often enough? You need to clean them out completely and change all of their bedding and litter every week, including making sure their toys are clean. You'll also need to do a spot clean every day, taking out any obvious soiling and wet bedding.

Chapter 3. Flying Squirrels as pets

Do you have enough space for a flying squirrel? They need a large enclosure and somewhere where they won't be disturbed too much. Ideally they would be kept in a spare room or an office that doesn't have people coming and going all of the time.

Will you be able to set up a room for them to play in that is flying squirrel proof? You need to be able to make sure they can play safely without risk of them getting stuck behind the piano or under the floorboards. This is very important so you don't spend the whole of play time fussing and worrying about where they are.

Can you meet their dietary requirement? They need fresh fruit and vegetables and clean grain every day, as well as some of the grimmer foods, like live and dried insects. They will need this attending to every day.

What would you do if they bit you? Could you cope with the idea that your lovely cute baby has hurt you on purpose? While the bite may not be vindictive it can really hurt your feelings when something you have nurtured their entire life breaks the trust and snaps at you. While unlikely, all animals can bite.

Do you have the time and patients to bond properly with your flying squirrel? If you don't have the time to spend with your flying squirrel it may be difficult to get them to bond to you and you may have problems in the future. Also, if you start out handling them every day but this drops off a bit, you could end up with a very unhappy, lonely pet.

Can you make a 10-15 year commitment to love and care for your flying squirrel? They can last a long time and will always require the same amount of love, time and patience.

Will you be ok with being messed and wee'd on? They will probably have a few accidents on you in their time. How much will this upset you?

Can you cope with a grumpy/huffy flying squirrel and keep up the daily handing and fussing to get them back to their sweet old self? That can be very important and can keep your flying squirrel at home and out of the animal shelter.

Despite all of this, flying squirrels are increasingly popular as pets. They are sweet and affectionate and the bond with their owner is so mutually rewarding that most people who have flying squirrels say they would get another once their current one passes away, despite all of the possible pitfalls and problems.

3. Costs

Initial costs

The initial costs of a flying squirrel could be more than you expect in itself.

Baby Formula ingredients.......$12/£8

Wire enclosure and accessories......$80-$240/£60-£300

Bag of food.....................$5-$15/£3-£10

Calcium Supplement.............$15/£10

Solid (not wire) wheel...........$20/£15

Bonding pouches................$8/£5

Misc. toys & accessories........$15/£10

This makes for a total outpay of up to $325 or £278, and that doesn't even include the price of your flying squirrel. Once you factor in this cost you could end up paying up to $550 or £478.

Monthly costs

This is only the beginning. The insurance could be up to $25 or £15 per month. They eat roughly $20 or £15 worth of food a month making the monthly costs <u>$45 or £30.</u>

First year

All of this could mean your first year outpay could be up to $1090 and $540 there after, or in the UK £838 and £360 per year after that. The cost of keeping these animals is not small, roughly the same as keeping and insuring a dog or cat.

4. Other animals

Animals introduced to each other at a young age can get along quite well. There are instances of pet flying squirrels playing quite happily with fancy rats, chinchillas, chipmunks, rabbits and even cats and dogs. One flying squirrel who's enclosure was in the same room as the owner's fancy rats developed a very close and affectionate relationship with the youngest rat to the point where they would sit for hours together in the pocket of their owner while they all watched TV together.

There is a story of a female Russian Giant flying squirrel who became very close with the female chinchilla in the next enclosure. They were such good friends that when the chinchilla fell and died a week after giving birth, the flying squirrel ended up nursing an orphaned chinchilla along with her own 3 week olds pups. There is a cute Youtube clip of a rabbit and a flying squirrel being "friends", though one gets the impression that there is more in it for the flying squirrel than the rabbit. There are lots of sweet stories about flying squirrels with pet dogs.

These are exceptions, however, and not the rule. There are many reasons for these animals to be naturally suspicious of each other. In the wild, rats and mice will predate on baby flying squirrels, making them naturally, and understandably, very suspicious of each other.

A chinchilla in the wild will rarely come into contact with flying squirrels as there are only wild chinchillas in Peru and Chile, but they would be in competition for food and can be aggressively territorial. Chipmunks share wild territories with flying squirrels in North America and Asia. While these animals pose no immediate threat in the wild, in close quarters they could become aggressive towards one another.

Rabbits can be a lot bigger and stronger than a flying squirrel and may harm the flying squirrel accidentally. On the other hand, an over amorous flying squirrel could hurt a docile rabbit in the excitement. It is also important to remember that while we may see our rabbit as sweet and gentle, they can become aggressive, and rabbits housed with guinea pigs, though they often get on fine, have been know to viciously savage their cage mates to death.

Cats and dogs, while they can get on well with small rodents, are more likely to see them as toys or prey. It is ill advised to let your flying squirrels out to play with these animals.

Under no circumstances house other animals in the same enclosure as your flying squirrel even if they get on really well. No animals are completely predictable.

5. Health benefits of flying squirrels

There have been ideas for years that pets are good for your
health. Stroking a cat or dog has a soothing affect and the
responsibility of pet ownership has a generally stabilizing effect
on mood and behavior. Studies have shown that owning a pet can
increase the levels of endorphins in the brain and can increase
physical health, improve sleep patterns and stave off illness. Pets
can reduce the symptoms of depression. The soothing, repetitive
action of stroking a pet has been proven to lower blood pressure.

How do Flying squirrels fit in with this?
Because of the closeness of the bond between a flying squirrel
and their owner, the love and affection shown can seriously
improve mood.

If you find yourself becoming isolated, pets, especially less
common ones, are really good icebreakers. By joining an owners'
forum and going to meetings, you can find that you have a
network of friends across the world.

Pets can really push you to social interaction in ways that you are
not being negatively judged. The depth of the bond between a
flying squirrel and it's people mean that they make great
companion animals.

It's strange, but even when you struggle to take care of yourself
emotionally, having a dependant who relies on you to get out of
bed and feed and cuddle "can help give you a sense of your own
value and importance", according to Dr Ian Cook, director of the
Depression Research (UCLA)

The uncomplicated nature of the bond between a flying squirrel and their owner can be a great antidote to complex family and social relationships.

Having a routine with your flying squirrel can add structure to your day and this is a fantastic way to keep your mental health on track.

Chapter 4. Caring for your Flying Squirrels

1. Housing requirements

Flying squirrels have very specific enclosure requirements, which are similar, though not identical, to other exotic pets, such as sugar gliders, Gambian pouched rats and chinchillas. They need space to jump about, things to climb on and toys to play with.

Some owners keep their flying squirrels out all the time and do not have a cage of any kind, though this is not advised as they are fairly small and can become trapped or injured easily if not supervised. Also, they can tend to chew wires. This wire chewing tendency, at best is annoying, but at worst it can be fatal to your pet, and it would be an excruciatingly painful way for your little friend to die.

It may seem a nice idea to have your flying squirrel sleep in your bed, though this can cause serious problems, as once again, they could become trapped or even be smothered, crushed or killed if you roll over in the night. The risk of waking up to find that you have crushed and killed your pet would be incredibly distressing for anyone.

Space and enclosure types:
While it's sometimes suggested that your flying squirrel will able to live in a 70cm or 27inch cube, this is not recommended and is considered quite cruel. In laboratory conditions, this is considered adequate, but by pet owners it is not, and as you will have the best interests of your pet at heart, you will want to consider something much more appropriate. They will be much happier

and healthier if they can move around. Provided with a large enclosure of about 60cm X 90cm X 150cm, which in inches is roughly 23 X 35 X 60, or bigger, your flying squirrel is much more likely to thrive. You can keep up to 3 flying squirrels in an enclosure of this size. For 4-6 flying squirrels, you want to be looking at something about half this size again and so on. In this environment your flying squirrel will be able to show more natural behaviours, move about more freely and generally be happier and healthier.

A lot of flying squirrel owners use enclosures that are meant for large birds, as these are nice and tall and allow their flying squirrels to jump about and climb. The only thing to watch for with bird enclosures is the bar spacing - you need to make sure your young flying squirrel can't escape. It is recommended that bar spacing be no more than 2cm; just under an inch.

Enclosures made specifically for chipmunks, chinchillas, ferrets and fancy rats are also good, as they provide good height for flying squirrels to climb about in and jump from place to place. Another advantage of a taller enclosure is that they don't take up much floor space for the amount of living space they provide. Something like the Aurora 600 or the larger Madrid enclosure would be great, as these are fairly robust and chew proof without being galvanised. The Miami ferret enclosure by Montana is very attractive and big enough. These are usually power coated and so should be safe.

If you want to really spoil your flying squirrel or perhaps want to breed, then the best enclosure is the Ferret and Chinchilla Tower Rise. This is a huge enclosure at 107cm X 58cm X 199cm or 42in X 23in X 78in. It can be divided up into 3 separate living quarters for separating the males off once the babies are born, or for slow introductions of new members to an existing group. This is available in the UK from www.cagesworld.co.uk priced £299 and the US equivalent is the Large X 3 Level Ferret Chinchilla Sugar Glider Cage from http://stores.ebay.com/Pets-Home-Professional-Products priced at $237. This enclosure is almost identical but doesn't come with partitions, though these can easily be made with sections of powder coated steel - talk to your local steel or metal dealer, as they may have off cuts that would suit your purposes.

All of these enclosures have large access doors. This is vitally important when choosing an enclosure, as it is a lot easier, comfier and safer to take your pet out through a large door. Large doors also make it easier to clean out and inspect the cage – you can usually get your shoulders through and this will make life a lot easier.

If you're looking at these new and thinking that they're expensive, then take a look on eBay, Craigslist, Gumtree and Preloved for second hand enclosures. Remember, what ever you decide, this is an investment for your pet's long-term happiness and they can live for up to 15 years in captivity, so buy the best quality and size of enclosure you can afford now to avoid expensive replacements and repairs in the future. If you give yourself time to look around and do your research into enclosures then you can get yourself a good deal, as well as being properly prepared. If you're not prepared and have to get an enclosure in a rush, you could find yourself paying more than you need to.

Whatever type of enclosure you go for, there are some important things to remember. Most enclosures available have wire bases to allow any mess to fall through into a removable tray. While this makes cleaning out easier, it can be very bad for your critter's feet. This doesn't mean that you need to cover the base. What it does mean is that you should have solid shelves where they can rest their feet. As flying squirrels are arboreal in nature, they will tend to spend most of their time off the floor anyway, if they are given the opportunity.

Avoid galvanized enclosures, as chewing the coating from these can lead to fatal zinc poisoning. While galvanisation is meant to prevent chewing, it doesn't always and heavy metal poisoning can occur fairly rapidly in smaller animals.

Should you have only one or a troop?
Because of the close bond that forms between a flying squirrel and its primary carers it is fine to keep just one flying squirrel, as they will not get lonely for their own kind if they have their owner instead. With many mammals it can be cruel to keep them in solidarity but flying squirrels bond so closely with those who handle them regularly that they do not need enclosure mates. If you do decide to get two, it is best to get two same sex babies of the same age unless you intend to breed. Even with two you can still get them to bond with you as they are social animals and have enough love to go round. If you do get more than one flying squirrel it is a good idea to have room for them to get away from each other if they need to, so multiple nest boxes are a must. While two flying squirrels don't need twice as much room as only one it is still vital that they do have more space.

Branches

Access to branches or some sort of climbing medium, no matter how small, is vital to the health and behavioural aspects of looking after your flying squirrel and should be a main feature of your enclosure decoration. You can get these from most pet stores

–java wood for example is readily available - or ask a friendly gardener or handy man to keep back any fruit tree clippings he has for you. They will usually be happy to do this as it saves them having to dispose of them.

Seashells

Seashells are fun to play with and they provide something to chew that is high in calcium so they are important to have in the enclosure. They can hang from the ceiling or be strewn about the enclosure floor.

Ropes

Another thing you definitely need in your enclosure is rope. There are lots of ideas later in the book about what to do with ropes, but they are essential.

Wheel

You are definitely going to need a wheel or silent spinner for your flying squirrel to exercise on. Full details are available later in the book.

Baby tank

You are going to need a baby tank or acclimatisation tank, used to get the animal used to its surroundings, but where it cannot hurt itself by climbing and falling. This may seem odd as they don't live in tanks, but when they are very young they can struggle to regulate their temperature. Having a baby tank for them to get used to their new home in is very comforting, though you will need to clean them out every day as the air won't circulate as well in a tank as in a wire or bar enclosure, and the build up of ammonia can be not only unpleasant, but dangerous. You will only want to keep your new baby in here for a couple of days, or until they have finished being syringe fed.

2. Feeding and treats

Nutritional needs of flying squirrels are not very difficult to meet if you know what to look for. Flying squirrels need a high protein, high calcium diet with high fibre as well as lots of fresh fruit and vegetables. Most of their protein and fibre should come from nuts and seeds as they are granivorous - grain eaters. The ideal feed for flying squirrels should contain a good range of fruit, vegetables, seeds, nuts, fruit tree barks, and insects. Your flying squirrel will eat about their body weight in food every 4 days. Saying this, they should always have access to more food, even if they've already eaten that much.

You also need to provide fresh drinking water. This should be in a gravity fed bottle like those available for rabbits and small rodents. Do not use water bowls, as there is a risk of aspirating or drowning with any real depth of water. If a human child can drown in an inch of water, a flying squirrel can drown in less. You need to change the water every few days or so, even if the bottle isn't empty, to keep it fresh and avoid the danger of the bacterial growth that can get out of control in stagnant water.

Feeding enrichment (playing with food like a child or a wild animal) is very important to the emotional health of your flying squirrel – it can reduce stress, encourage movement and fitness, keep the brain active and reduce boredom. They need to be able to exhibit natural foraging behaviour, and a great way to get them to do this is to make their food into part of a challenge or game. You'll have been told not to play with your food as a child; well this is your chance to make food fun again, though I don't advise you to share your flying squirrel's dinner. One really good, easy way to do this is to drill large holes in their branches, and stuff their food into the holes so that they have to both climb and dig for their dinner. It is also good to hide food around the enclosure for your flying squirrel to hunt for. For other enrichment ideas you can look at the toys and games sections of this book. Your flying squirrels should also have a base of some sort of unhomogenised squirrel pellets or a mixed complete, seed based squirrel food. If you can't get hold of squirrel food, a good quality, unhomogenised rabbit food will be just as good. Do not use homogenised food, as this restricts the natural tendency for selective browsing.

A homogenised food has been mashed and mixed so much that the food is all the same, and then reconstructed. It will be pellets of a brownish green colour and they will all have the same content. An unhomogenised food is not reconstructed and will contain grass pellets, flakes of carrot, pea or sweet corn and grains.

While this means that you can't make sure your pets eat all of their 'complete' pet food, it does also mean that your flying squirrel can eat based on its nutritional needs as opposed to what the food manufacturers decide they need, some semblance of control over diet and environment is very important to the mental health of your flying squirrel – you'd be depressed if you couldn't even decide what to have for dinner. Most importantly of all, you should supplement this with treats. They should have a variety of different treats on different days. Don't go over board here, they'll be getting used to a lot of new things when they first arrive with you so they don't need every type of treat mentioned straight away. Try them with one new thing a week to keep them interested.

Nuts and seeds

They love nuts. Acorns, pecans, walnuts, beach nuts and the like are all very good for flying squirrels. They provide a good source of fat, oils and proteins, which make for healthy coats and muscle tone. Any food safe seeds are good for your flying squirrel for the same reasons. They are particularly partial to sunflower seeds. They can also eat unsweetened cereals and wholemeal bread crusts.

Though incredibly high in fat, almonds are very good, healthy treats because of their high phosphorous content, which helps with strong bones and teeth. Almonds are among the few nuts that alkalize the body; improving immune response. Almonds reduce cholesterol, reduce blood pressure, reduce the risk of weight gain and reduce the risk of heart problems.

One of nature's super-foods, sunflower seeds, are a fantastic source of nutrition, containing over 80 nutrients. They are full of vitamin E, which protects cell membranes and brain cells and stop cholesterol oxidising and becoming a problem. The high magnesium content of sunflower seeds lowers blood pressure. Magnesium also stops vital calcium from blocking the nerves, so it can be used elsewhere by the body. The selenium in sunflower seeds drastically reduces the risk of some cancers.

As a serious super seed, sesame seeds are a real health booster for your flying squirrel. Lowering blood pressure, preventing diabetes and inhibiting the growth of cancer, you might want to eat these yourself. They are seriously good for your pet.

It may seem odd but walnuts can protect against naturally occurring chemicals that can cause cancers and other diseases.

Cashews contain very strong flavenoids that starve cancerous tumours. The high magnesium content helps calcium to strengthen bones, which is excellent in flying squirrels.

Another high-density nutrient nut is the pecan. They are packed full of anti-oxidants and vitamins. The high protein content makes them good for flying squirrels.

Pine nuts are such a big part of the wild diet of the flying squirrel for a really good reason. Because of their nocturnal nature, flying squirrels have very little natural vitamin D, but luckily, their coniferous forest home is high in pine seeds and pine seeds are full of vitamin D.

High in protein, anti-oxidants and omega3 fatty acids, flax seed have the most nutrients for their size of any grain in the world. One of the great things about flax is that it is easy to grow and has very pretty blue flowers.

Insects

Insects and their larvae make wonderful treats for flying squirrels. They are a really good source of goodness and they generally contain 55%-85% moisture.

The problem with a lot of insects is that they contain little calcium but the calcium content of wax worms, house crickets, mealworms and silkworms can all be increased 5 to 20-fold when fed a high calcium diet. Lots of insects bred for food have higher calcium content due to their diets.

As most insects seem to be good sources of lots of good trace minerals such as iron, zinc, copper, manganese and selenium, this means they shouldn't need any supplements of these useful minerals. Insects also have a really good amino acid content and the uptake of amino acids from insects is quite high, between 45% and 90%. All of the insects listed here are available from one of there various online suppliers listed at the back of this book.

Live meal worms are very nutritious and can make such a good enrichment for your flying squirrel. They are available frozen and dry if you're a bit squeamish. Live meal worms hidden in sand, coir or sphagnum moss are a delicious and fun treat that keep your flying squirrel on their toes.

Crickets make a much better addition of calcium than calcium powder and flying squirrels do need additional calcium in their diet to keep their bones and health strong. If you're planning to feed live crickets there are silent breeds available. Live crickets can hop about a bit and if the bars of the enclosure are too far apart, they can get everywhere. If you provide a hide box for them inside the enclosure, they will go in there and are less likely to escape, hop about your living room and breed uncontrollably under the sofa or behind the TV.

Ants are a fantastic source of protein and are tasty baked, squashed into other food or stirred into the main food. Ants should not be fed live as they can get everywhere, no matter which safeguards you put in place and don't make very pleasant house guests.

Mopani worms are a real treat for anyone and are eaten as a snack in many parts of Africa- they taste a bit like salami and have a delightful crunchy/fatty bacon texture. These are another excellent source of protein and are very good for their muscles. These should only be given as an occasional treat and should be stored well in the freezer.

Waxworms are often very sweet, as they're usually fed on honey and wheat germ and make a good occasional treat, but due to the high sugar and fat content you may want to log when these have been given, especially if you are not the only one who treats your flying squirrel.

The Dubai cockroach is much smaller than those horrid things you find scuttling across your cringe worthiest nightmares and unhygienic restaurants, and they make a delicious treat for your flying squirrel. They are high in protein, calcium and minerals.

Any spiders that find their way into your flying squirrels enclosure will have to watch out as flying squirrels love spiders and will gobble them up happily. Slugs and snails are not only an excellent source of calcium and protein but if they're from your garden and you don't use poisons they are a useful free treat.

Chapter 4. Caring for your Flying Squirrels

Tree, shrub and plant material

Most of the salad foods we eat, our flying squirrels can eat too.

Tomatoes hidden around the enclosure make a great treat. The skin is a nice tearing challenge in itself, then the squishy tasty flesh and inside there's a lovely crunchy seedy bit.

Cabbage is high in vitamins and minerals, the most important of these being iron. A cabbage leaf can be good enrichment, as it has a tough, veined texture, making it a bit of a challenge to tear.

High in calcium, iron and water content, spinach is a great food for your flying squirrel.

Peas and beans make a fantastic addition to any diet, when dried they're good for your flying squirrel's teeth. When fresh they're a good source of vitamins and minerals.

Broccoli is so high in calcium that it's an absolute must for flying squirrels. They don't need massive amounts, but if you keep a bit back before you cook it for yourself and your family, then little florets will not only be a welcome treat, but also very good for the long term health of your flying squirrel as it also contains all of the other good things you'd expect from a green vegetable.

It's not just broccoli that's a great green - kale and Swiss chard are packed full of goodness, containing high levels of vitamins and minerals, including the vital calcium.

This next suggestion is going to seem a bit indulgent, but if you're looking for a nice, high fat high protein treat, then the odd artichoke is a great little occasional treat.

Chapter 4. Caring for your Flying Squirrels

Fruit is very important to the diet of the flying squirrel. In the wild, as opportunistic omnivorous feeders, flying squirrels will happily scoff down fruits.

To protect against cancers and boost immune systems you need to feed your flying squirrel something high in anti-oxidants and vitamin C, such as small amounts of blueberries, strawberries and kiwis.

Fruits that are readily available dried are useful if you need to go away and can't feed fresh fruit every day. Dried apples, pears, pineapple and bananas are some of the fruits that retain their nutritional values the best.

Figs are the fruit with the highest calcium content and make a really nice present for your flying squirrel as they also have a very high sugar content.

Oranges have a good lot of the vital calcium needed for your flying squirrel's health.

Do not feed them lettuce, as this can be poisonous to small animals and can cause fatal diarrhoea. They like maple bark and leaves and are incredibly fond of young maple swigs and shoots. Raw cauliflower and other brasiccas like cabbage and broccoli are always appreciated. A lot of weeds are good for them too. All over the world, dandelions grow in inconvenient places. If you can find dandelions that haven't been treated with any pesticide, they make a delicious treat for flying squirrels and are high in iron and zinc. In North America edible milkweed and Solomon's seal are common and can be eaten by flying squirrels. In the UK Japanese knotweed is a real pest, growing rampantly in neatly manicured gardens and destroying all sense of order, but is edible and can be fed to flying squirrels.

Other

Flying squirrels eat most fruits and berries, apple and orange slices especially. Any fungi we can eat, they can eat. They love eggs, but because of the high cholesterol, your flying squirrel should only be given egg very occasionally, but a hard-boiled egg, complete in shell, can be real fun to get into and can add lots of important enrichment and natural behaviours for your flying squirrel. They can also have very small amounts of honey or maple syrup, but not too much as this is bad for their health.

Calcium is a must for flying squirrels and while there are lots of ways to get calcium into their diet, it is a good idea to keep a log of what high calcium foods they have been given so that you can check to make sure they've had enough. Crickets, figs, orange slices and cuttlefish are all good sources of calcium but calcium supplements are available if you're worried about your flying squirrel's dietary calcium intake.

3. Useful websites for buying housing, food and treats

Housing

http://www.viovet.co.uk

http://www.monsterpetsupplies.co.uk

www.superpetusa.com

www.onlinepetdepot.com

www.smallanimalchannel.com

Toys

chinchillatoys.com

www.chinnieshop.com

www.chinchillas2shop.co.uk/

www.littlepetwarehouse.co.uk

www.petplanet.co.uk

www.home2roost.co.uk

www.ratwarehouse.com

www.rataccessories.co.uk/

www.rattoy.com

Food

http://www.exoticnutrition.com

edible.com

http://www.livefoodsdirect.co.uk

livefoodonline.com/

livefood.co.uk/

livefoodsbypost.co.uk/

www.reptiles.swelluk.com

www.petsathome.com

http://www.trau-dich-shop.com/

www.naturesgrub.co.uk/
www.expeditionfoods.com/DriedMeals

Chapter 5. Settling in your baby

1. Bonding

The strength of the way that these animals bond is one of the reasons that they can make such good pets and the closeness of the bond is unique among exotic rodents. They imprint on their humans like a hand reared bird. A baby flying squirrel who is hand reared properly by a kind human will love them unconditionally for the rest of it's life. Bonding happens during the first few weeks of your flying squirrel living with you and should last for the animal's entire life.

Like all young mammals, baby flying squirrels find closeness to something bigger or very comforting. You should carry your baby in a bonding pouch (see chapter 7) or your shirt pocket. In fact, many owners use a 'squirrel hoody' which is only worn when handling their flying squirrel and the mixed scent is never washed off. The reason this carrying around is so important, especially in young flying squirrels is that when they are close to your body they can use your body heat to regulate their temperature and they can hear your blood whooshing around your body. This is very similar to the sound the baby would have heard in the mother's womb and like all baby mammals, it is very comforting to them - it is like making shooshing sounds to a baby human.

You should aim to have your flying squirrel out with you for at least an hour a day. You should also try to play games with your flying squirrel; in the evening when they are most active is best, and again you should try to play with them for about an hour a day.

One of the most important things that marks out the flying squirrel above other pet animals is the way that they bond with you, and nothing shows this bond like 'hypnotizing' your flying squirrel. This can also be done with rabbits and ferrets. If you hold your animal close, in the crook of your arm and look into each others eyes the bond is obvious. You need one hand/arm under the body along the back and the other laid over the tummy so that you can reach the face with the hand. Stroke the face firmly over the bridge of the nose just below the eye sockets. The light pressure around the scent glands is incredibly soothing and relaxing, some people refer to this as hypnotism, though the animal is simply very relaxed and sleepy. If they are used to it, you can use this technique to calm your pet when they are distressed, to examine them after a fall, or at vet visits. It is so useful to be able to calm your flying squirrel when you need to. It is also a lovely bonding experience.

Another popular way to gain your baby's trust is to hand feed. This will make the baby imprint on you and the animal will learn to always love to be around you.

Hand-Feeding

In order to bond with your flying squirrel it is recommend that you hand feed them when they first get to you. The instructions for the formula are in the back of this book, in the chapter about breeding. You have to be very careful doing this, as improper hand feeding can cause a fatal aspiration. This is where the milk is aspirated into the lungs and can make your flying squirrel ill, or even kill it. If you are not confident about this it is possible to get them at up to 9 weeks and still bond with them properly. From 7 weeks on they are much less dependant.

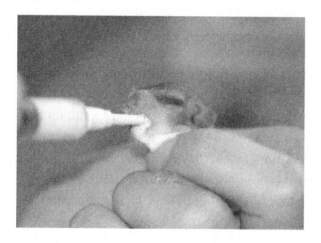

Most private breeders and hobby breeders will have bottle fed the baby already, even if this is just topping up what the mother was giving, as this makes it easier for the mother as well as future owners. As a result, when you receive your baby it may well already be accustomed to being hand-fed and will probably be ready to eat when it gets home. If you have your baby shipped to you by courier instead of collecting it yourself, you should make up the formula *before* you get them out of their carrier. You'll need to have a paper towel or some kitchen roll ready to wipe the face as milk can be a real irritant and can cause excessive grooming and hair loss. This is a very bad habit for your baby to get into.

You should use a small syringe, of about 5ml. You don't need to use a different syringe for each feed, but you do need to clean them before and after every use. Do not use bleach or detergent to do this.

To feed your baby, get the baby out of the carrier or enclosure and set it down. Do not feed your baby on its back. Under no circumstances should a baby be fed on its back. This is so dangerous and I can't stress enough how careful you must be.

Baby flying squirrels fed on their backs can, and usually will, die of aspiration pneumonia or just straight out drown on milk. Show them the tip of the syringe. They should know what it is if they've been hand reared at all before, and put their mouth up to it. Now, as slowly as you can, push the plunger, stopping every few seconds to let them finish what they have in their mouths. Once again, I can't stress enough that this must be done as slowly as you can, aspirating the milk could kill your baby within hours. It should take about ten minutes. There is a video on youtube, http://www.youtube.com/watch?v=Uz3_2bHtbWw of a baby flying squirrel, who died from drowning. He ate his milk too fast. If you aren't sure how slow to go, have a look at this video to get an idea. This is one of the very good reasons not to use a pipette, as the baby can guzzle down as much as he wants, and hungry baby flying squirrels don't know their limits.

You should feed your baby three to six times a day, more if your baby is hungry. Each feed should be about fifteen to twenty five ml, but if your flying squirrel isn't hungry don't force them to have more than they want. After feeding your baby, you should set them down somewhere they can rest - preferably in their nest or in their enclosure - to digest. Try to let them have an hour.

2. Preparing for your flying squirrel

This is a handy list of things you will need to take care of your flying squirrel

Baby Formula ingredients
Wire enclosure and accessories
Acclimatisation or baby tank
Bag of food
Some treats
Calcium Supplement
Solid (not wire) wheel
Bonding pouches
Toys
A log book

Log book

A lot of people who own exotic pets have an out of date week per page diary that they use to keep track of their animal's habits, as these can be picked up very cheaply from stationers mid year. The idea of a log book may seem over the top and perhaps even a little obsessive, but log books are a real asset to keeping your flying squirrel healthy. If there is more than one care-giver a log book can help to keep the care consistent and make the communication clear and open.

Your log book should have one page per week. You should record any vet visits or medications your pet is given. The top line should have the week beginning date, the weight of the flying squirrel at the last weigh in and the average weight of your flying squirrel. The rest of the page should have two columns, each split into 7 rows.

One column should be for food, what, exactly, have they been given to eat that day? Did they eat it, store it or ignore it? This is so useful to make sure they've had all of the things they need each week. If there is more than one person responsible for feeding, this system is especially useful as it means that calcium isn't missed and fatty foods aren't over fed.

The other column should be for notes on their behaviour that day. Have they been more or less affectionate than usual? Has there been an incident that upset them? Were there any other animals, or unusual smells or things in the room? How did they respond? This is really handy for assessing and diagnosing any behavioural problems.

If you keep good notes about your pets eating and behavioural patterns it is really easy to pin point anything that changes. You should also keep a note of any changes in the way your pet moves as well as any falls or knocks. This can be instrumental in noticing if there is anything physically wrong with your pet. As flying squirrels are not common pets, any information about the specific normal behaviour and changes in patterns of your flying squirrel can be very useful to a vet if anything goes wrong.

Chapter 6. Health

1. Common health conditions

While there have been no reported cases of rabies in flying squirrels, they are still classed as wild animals if they are wild caught and wild caught pet flying squirrels can be killed if they bite someone. They can get typhus, though it is very rare that this is passed on to people. They can get lice, fleas, mites and parasites.

Lice, fleas, mites and parasites
Parasites and blood sucking nasties in the fur of wild flying squirrels can be a real problem. They can cause toxicity and anaemia. Due to their small size, blood loss on any scale can make a flying squirrel very ill. Paleness in the skin of the gums is a clear sign of anaemia; any anaemia should be treated with a small amount of a diluted iron solution in their water, or lots fresh spinach. As always, if the symptoms persist or if you're worried in any way about this, you need to take your flying squirrel to the vet.

It is very unlikely that a pet flying squirrel will get any parasites, fleas, mites or ticks as they shouldn't come into contact with any carriers of these sorts of things. They certainly shouldn't come into contact with wild flying squirrels. This would be disastrous and you should never let this happen. Wild animals carry specific illnesses and creepy crawlies that can do your pet real damage. The wild populations tend to have better immunity and can carry pathogens and diseases without showing any symptoms.

If you have other pets that go outside, dogs or cats for example, you need to try to avoid their contact with wild flying squirrels too, as they could carry all sorts of horrid things in with them. If your cat or dog catches a wild flying squirrel, disinfect everything it comes into contact with (not the dog or cat, obviously) and bathe your pet to get rid of any parasites or germs.

Pets that go outdoors can carry biting insects from outdoors, but are generally not in very close contact with either wild or pet flying squirrels. A cat may occasionally take a wild flying squirrel. If your pet cat does take a wild flying squirrel you need to be careful about contamination. Disinfect any surfaces that the corpse comes into contact with and quarantine your cat away from your pet flying squirrel for at least 3 weeks. Nothing carried by the wild flying squirrel should affect your cat as their biology is very different and as long as your cat is up to date with it's flee and worm treatments there should be no problem.

Anything taking nutrients from something so small as your flying squirrel can cause problems very quickly. Most of these conditions are easily treatable with over the counter medicines. Lice, fleas and mites can be treated with a simple topical treatment. Do not use medicines intended for cats or dogs, as these will be meant for use on much larger animals with greater tolerances. You can use flea treatments meant for smaller mammals such as small rabbits and chipmunks.

The lice that affect flying squirrels again tend not to be an issue in captive bred flying squirrels, but you do need to keep an eye out for the thin bodied, flightless insects as it is lice that can spread typhus to people.

Fleas that like flying squirrels aren't usually able to get into your home, as they're not generally carried by other, free roaming pets, such as cats or dogs. You do need to treat any fleas as soon as you see them, however, as there are fleas that can transmit typhus to humans from flying squirrels.

Orchopeas howardii is the flea that transmits typhus.

The mites that affect flying squirrels are not very pleasant, but generally don't bother the captive bred populations. The mites they can get are:

Psorergates glaucomys
Euhaemogamasus ambulans
Trembicula micrati
Haemolaelaps megaventralis
Haemogamasus reidi
Androlaelaps fahrenholzi

Malocclusion of the teeth

A malocclusion of the teeth can be incredibly painful. The pain can stop the animal eating and cause serious malnourishment. Worse than the pain, if the teeth rub the lips and gums they can make cuts, which can bleed or become infected. If the lower teeth protrude to the side, they can cause cuts and infections to the face, or worse, damage the eye. Any damage to the eye will be irreparable and there have been cases of flying squirrels loosing eyes through a malocclusion of the teeth that could have been rectified by a couple of trips to the vet, or a tooth file and maintenance regime implemented early on.

Calcium deficiency

As flying squirrels are nocturnal and don't get exposed to UV, a key factor in calcium absorption as it gives off vitamin D3, they are incurably prone to calcium deficiency. One of the horrifying symptoms of this is that their hind legs can become paralysed. If this happens you need to take your flying squirrel to a vet immediately! This is an emergency situation. If you don't have a vet you can get to immediately, phone them (if it is safe and legal to do so,) for advice on your way to them. This is fairly easy to avoid, however, as you can make sure your flying squirrel has a high calcium diet (see diet and treats and diets to keep your flying squirrel healthy).

Chapter 6. Health

Obesity

Obesity in something so small may seem laughable, but it can be a real problem. Because of their tiny stature, their tolerances to weight gain are far finer than in larger animals. Obesity can cause bone defects, heart problems and can put undue stress on their little organs. If your flying squirrel had access to enough exercise and stimulation then becoming over weight is unlikely, but you still need to monitor their weight with weekly weigh ins and record this in their log book.

Diarrhoea

Diarrhoea can kill. It kills children in Africa. It kills the small and the sick all over the world and it kills rodents and small mammals in a very short space of time. If your flying squirrel gets diarrhoea and becomes dehydrated you need to get it to a vet ASAP.

You can tell if an animal is dehydrated by lifting their skin between your fingers. If the skin returns to the body quickly, if it pings or snaps back then the situation isn't too dangerous. If the skin stays away from the body for any length of time then you have a dehydration problem.

Dehydration is more dangerous than starvation and you need to get some fluids in immediately and get to the vets. This is where keeping hold of some of the hand feeding things from when it was a baby may come in handy. If there is no vet available or you can't get an emergency appointment and have to wait an hour or so it is important to get some fluids into your flying squirrel. A rehydration and anti diarrhoea solution carefully administered could save your flying squirrel's life.

What you need

Imodium or similar product
Salt
Water
Sugar
A 1-2ml syringe

What you do

Mix ¼ of a teaspoon of Imodium with a pinch of salt and a pinch of sugar into 10ml of warm (not hot or cool) water. Fill the syringe with the solution and, holding your flying squirrel upright, (never feed on their back) slowly feed it some of the solution. It is vital that you do this very slowly. It may seem counter intuitive because of the urgency of the situation, but you have to do this very slowly as an aspiration could kill your flying squirrel just as quickly as the dehydration you're trying to solve. If your flying squirrel isn't swallowing don't try to force feed, as this could also cause an aspiration and any liquid at all on such tiny lungs can be fatal.

Some rabbit and rat owners rehydrate their pets with emergency enemas using the same solution as the lower bowel can absorb water, though I don't recommend this except in extreme emergencies, (i.e. your vet is 5 hours drive away).

A less invasive way to do this is to submerse your flying squirrel's back end in warm water, though you have to be very careful not to let them cool down afterwards, as this could cause a fatal torpor.

2. How to tell if your flying squirrel is under the weather

It can be incredibly hard to tell if your flying squirrel is at all unwell. All wild prey animals are expert in looking healthy when they are not – this is a vital survival strategy. Looking unwell or weak in any way is an invitation to predators, as they look for the weakest and easiest to catch to avoid expending too much of their own energy.

There are some signs you can look out for but you have to keep a watch of their health very closely to notice any change in your flying squirrel. This is one main reason that log books are so important.

Weight loss

As wild prey animals are in so much more danger from predators if they show any signs of weakness, they tend to be very good at hiding any symptoms they may have. This is true of most animals, but especially arboreal creatures, as, if they start to feel week or faint they could easily fall to their death. With these animals, weight loss is often the only sign that something is wrong.

One of the key indicators of poor health is weight loss. You should weigh your flying squirrel about once a week and keep a log of its weight. You need to find out the average weight of the breed you're getting and be aware of this when your flyer reaches adulthood. The breeder should be able to tell you about the weight of the parents and any older siblings. This way you can tell if your baby is growing and once they're fully grown it is easy to show if your flying squirrel is maintaining weight. Weight loss could be an indicator of something sinister.

If, for any reason, your animal isn't eating or can't eat, then they need to go to the vet. A flying squirrel can die of malnutrition in 75 hours. Also, if you've kept a log this could be a useful tool for your vet. If your flying squirrel looses weight you need to contact your vet who should be able to advise you on the next step.

Temperature change

While I don't suggest you try to take your flying squirrel's temperature, it is important to know their normal temperature. If you're handling your flying squirrel often enough, then this comes quite naturally. If you find any change, warm or cold, you should contact your vet immediately. If your flying squirrel is very cold you should try to warm them up – do not use radiators or hot water bottles. Simply pop them down your top so that they can use your temperature to regulate their own. This is where a strong bond is important. If they are very warm then fan them a little. If the temperature stays abnormal go to the vet.

If your flying squirrel becomes cold and unresponsive, this could be a form of torpor, and needs immediate veterinary attention. On the journey to the vets, keep your flying squirrel warm with your own body heat and do not use hot water bottles or other excessive heat sources.

Suddenly becoming timid

A usually outgoing flying squirrel that suddenly becomes timid could be hiding some other sign of distress or injury. Try to calm it by holding it close to you in a secure but not tight grip, or in a bonding pouch. Once your flying squirrel is calm, stroke them all over and be on the lookout for signs of pain or distress. If you find any, seek veterinary advice. This could also be a sign of something more sinister. Fear of people it normally finds comforting could signify some sort of brain injury or mental health problem.

3. Grooming and health

Nails

Your flying squirrel may need you to clip it's nails. If they don't wear them away properly while they're clambering about their enclosure and climbing their branches, the nails may get too long. Long claws can push the finger bones into strange shapes, get caught in things or curl up and hurt the feet. This is really a 2 person job. One of you needs to calm your flying squirrel and hold them firmly but gently so that they feel safe and secure. Then the other person should hold the paw in one hand, making sure that the flying squirrel can't kick out and cause an accident. Using a pain free, animal claw clippers, take the claw in the hole and clip. Be careful only to cut the tip so that you don't cut too much, as this can make the toes bleed. If you're worried about doing this then you can provide a scratch patch by gluing a piece of sand paper to a branch. Alternatively, you can ask your vet to clip the nails for you.

Teeth

If your flying squirrel has a malocclusion of the teeth, if they don't line up, then you need to get the teeth clipped or filled to prevent cuts, infections and ulcers. The teeth must be trimmed by a vet, as doing this wrong can cause the teeth to twist or splinter. You can file the teeth down, but this can be quite stressful and you need to decide if you want your flying squirrel to associate you with the experience of filing.

Fur and skin

Your flying squirrel will be able to groom their own fur quite well, but you need to get involved when things are stuck in the fur. You don't need to bath flying squirrels, but you do need to keep an eye out to make sure the fur is clean. If it isn't, brush it out with a nail brush or something similar, as the bristles aren't likely to damage the skin. You should check for any patches or skin problems every time you handle your flying squirrel and this daily check will allow you to nip any problems in the bud.

4. When to take your flying squirrel to the vet

Behavioural changes

Any sudden change in behaviour in your flying squirrel could be a sign that something isn't right. If you don't know why your flying squirrel is behaving differently, then you need to go to the vet. This is where good communication between all care givers and well kept records can come in really handy - if you have a "norm" to compare to it is a lot easier to spot when something is out of the ordinary.

Becoming unresponsive

If, for any reason, your flying squirrel becomes unresponsive to you or seems disorientated in anyway- it's time to seek veterinary advice.

Thirst or hunger

If your flying squirrel hasn't had a drink in 24 hours, or eaten in 72 hours, you need to go to the vet. If you keep a record of water given and daily levels then you can become aware much more quickly of anything abnormal. This is another advantage of the log book, tedious as it may be, it can literally, be a life saver. Excessive thirst can also be a sign of diabetes, so go to the vet.

Weight loss

If you notice any weight loss, at any stage, except in a female that has given birth, then this could be a sign of something nasty and you should take your flying squirrel to the vet. If you can present the vet with a record of weight and diet then this will save a lot of time and ambiguity.

Poison

If your flying squirrel finds itself with access to any sort of poison, the chances are that it will eat it – what can go wrong will go wrong. Go to the vet immediately. Do not pass go, do not collect $200, this is emergency territory. Take all of the information you have about the poison with you, if you have the packaging, take the packaging. Phone the vet for advice on the way there as they may recommend inducing vomiting or ingesting carbon. Inducing vomiting may be difficult with flying squirrels as they are technically classed as nonemetic (unable to throw up), though they have been known to, and vets do have tricks.

Seizure

If your flying squirrel has any sort of seizure, no matter how small, go to the vet. A seizure can look like a small sudden collapse, which seems quickly recovered from or it can be a collapse followed by a worrying time of incapacity and possibly shaking. Most animals suffering from a seizure will evacuate their bowels.

Strange movement

Any stiffness in your flying squirrels gait could be a sign of calcium deficiency beginning to cause paralysis. Take your flying squirrel to the vets.

If your flying squirrel develops any sort of wobbly gait, if they begin to move or stand strangely, seek veterinary attention – go to the vet.

Fur loss

If you notice fur loss this could be a sign of pest infestation, skin infection or stress. All of these things are dangerous to your pet. Go to the vet.

Lumps and bumps

If you feel an abnormal lump, it isn't necessarily cancer, but you need to seek immediate veterinary help, as even a benign fat lump can make your flying squirrel uncomfortable or ill.

Bleeding

Any profuse bleeding, obviously, needs to be seen by the vet. A little scratch will usually be ok, but even a small cut can become infected and an infection needs to be treated by the vet.

Broken bones

This is very obvious but any serious injury or wound, or any broken bones, need urgent veterinary attention.

Discharge from the eyes or nose

If you notice any sort of discharge from the nose or eyes, your flying squirrel needs to go to the vet. Any crusting of snot around the eyes or nose counts as a discharge.

If you're not sure whether you should take your flying squirrel to the vet, it's always better to be safe than sorry, so just take them. Your vet will understand and it could be useful. Even if there is no immediately life threatening situation, taking your flying squirrel to the vet because 'something is wrong' could allow your vet to find, treat or prevent a longer term underlying problem. This is where your log book will come in really handy, as you have a record of any changes.

5. Diets to keep your flying squirrel healthy

The most important thing your flying squirrel needs in its diet is calcium. Calcium deficiency in flying squirrels can be absolutely devastating, causing paralysis of the back legs. To avoid this horrifying problem, you can feed the high calcium foods listed for you in the food section.

A diet high in fresh fruit and vegetables is essential to keep your flying squirrel healthy. The vitamins and minerals in fresh fruit and vegetables keep the teeth, bones skin and fur of your flying squirrel strong and healthy. They also keep the immune system strong and make it easier for the body to fight off parasites.

6. Finding a vet

One of the most important things to do before anything goes wrong is to find a vet. The best way to find yourself a vet is to join exotics forums on the Internet and ask local owners about their experiences. You don't need a specifically trained flying squirrel vet – there's no such thing – but it does help if you find an exotic mammal's vet. Generally, small animal vets will be able to treat your flying squirrel, but you should ask them if they know any more specific vets. It could be that the vet you've been taking your dog to for years has a special interest in flying squirrels and is a secret expert. If not interested themselves, they may know a local vet who is. If you find a vet in the phone book and you've phoned up to check they're ok with flying squirrels you should look for reviews online.

Chapter 7. Play and enrichment

1. Games

Game playing is a vitally important tool for social, physical and mental learning and growth. As with human children, your flying squirrel will learn everything they know and most of their skills from you. Playing games helps to develop their social interaction skills and positive interactions with people will teach them that playing with people is fun. As your flying squirrel will still be very young, you will be responsible for much of their physical development, and playing games and training them will encourage a strong body, less liable to infection and damage. Playing finding, seeking and foraging games not only helps them to develop mentally but also teaches them how to work things out and encourages learning.

A great game that is easy to set up is hide and seek. Once you know what your flying squirrel's favourite food is you can hide it in little cardboard boxes or toilet role tubes. They also love assault courses with treats along them, hidden in clever little devices.

Seeing as wild squirrels get so much exercise clambering about in tree branches and up tree trunks, it is a good idea to let them have access to something similar in captivity, as this makes excellent enrichment, as well as being great for building muscle tone.

It would be ideal if they could have branches or someone similar to play with when they are having 'outside time'. The best situation would be if there are a flying squirrel "proof" rooms where your flying squirrel could just run wild for a little while.

As flying squirrels will make nests to sleep in, they instinctively enjoy gathering nesting material. Tissues make a great soft bed and can also make a fabulous game. Simply lay out a few tissues on a table or on the sofa and your flying squirrel will come and gather them all up, taking them all to the same place. Once they've got three of four piled up, you can start taking tissues off the pile and laying them out to be found and gathered again. This can keep your flying squirrel entertained for ages!

It may sound strange, but rodents can play peek-a-boo, and many flying squirrels love this game. Simply hide behind a book or ring binder and they'll come and find you. This is one of the most ridiculously cute games you will ever see!

Pea fishing is wonderful fun! A shallow bowl of water with some peas in is all you need. Your flying squirrel needs to be supervised playing this game, but they will love it. You can also float nuts and seeds in the bowl to mix it up a bit.

As flying squirrels are incredibly intelligent, they can learn to play other games. If you've got enough time and patience, you can teach your flying squirrel to play fetch.

What you need:
A ping pong ball
Some treats

What you do:
Drill holes in the ball to make it easier for your flying squirrel to handle. If your pet doesn't seem very interested in the ball, you can stuff it with a piece of something tasty and sticky like a bit of dried fig. Then, offer the ball to your flying squirrel and take it off them again very gently. Reward them as soon as the ball is in your hand again. Offer the ball again and once they've taken it,

hold out your hand for it back. If your flying squirrel doesn't give it back, take it off them again. Reward as soon as you have the ball back. Do this until your flying squirrel learns that giving you the ball means a treat. Then you need to place the ball on the ground. When your flying squirrel picks it up they should bring the ball to you for a treat. Then start placing the ball further and further away from you, treating every time it is returned. Eventually you will be able to throw the ball a short way and it will be brought back.

Another great game is not quite basket ball, where you can teach your flying squirrel to take a ball from one glass and drop it into another.

What you need:
A ping pong ball
2 tumbler glasses
Some treats

What you do:
Drill some holes in the ball to make it easy for your flying squirrel to pick up with its mouth or hands. If your flying squirrel shows no interest in the ball, try putting a sticky treat, like a piece of dried fig, inside the ball. Then, lay one of the glasses on its side with the ball at the bottom end so that your flying squirrel can get to the ball easily and retrieve it. Every time the ball is retrieved, give a little treat reward. Now increase the angle of the glass gently, letting the flying squirrel retrieve the ball each time, until the glass is upright and it will climb onto the glass in order to reach the ball at the bottom of it.

When your flying squirrel is doing this part of the game/ trick confidently, place the other glass next to the one with the ball.

When your flying squirrel retrieves the ball you can turn the glass that they're standing on so they are facing the other glass. Now, offer the treat over the other glass and they will drop the ball to accept it, hopefully the ball will fall into the glass. Repeat this until you feel your flying squirrel has the hang of it. Eventually, you need to stop offering the treat until the ball has already been dropped into the glass. Then you can move the glass further away.

One useful thing to remember is that flying squirrels are very clever and inquisitive. Any games that chinchillas, mice and rats can play, flying squirrels can play too. If you look on youtube or other pet forums there are lots of fantastic ideas and funny videos.

2. Toys

Toys are an important part of play and enrichment for your flying squirrel and can keep them entertained if you are away. Many flying squirrel owners don't feed their pets from food bowls at all, only feeding them from toys. There are so many toys available commercially and you can make toys for them too. There are some ideas of the toys you can buy and make below. A good place to look is in chinchilla, chipmunk, rat or even parrot forums, as pet owner are always eager to share their successes with each other, so that everyone's pet can be just as happy, though they do get competitive about who gives their pet the best quality time, the most fun toys and the healthiest tasty treats. Most of these pet forums have a toys and treats section that can point you to the right places and online shops to find what you're looking for, or if you just ask for ideas about toys in a new thread you could end up with a great long list of toys, shops and instructions.

a) Bought toys

Chapter 7. Play and enrichment

There are some wonderful toys available online, especially if you venture into toys designed for rats, dogs and parrots, as these tend to be robust and gnaw safe. You can find websites that these toys are available from at the end of this chapter.

Treat balls

Treat balls are fantastic things that can be filled with treats or food and then have the opening partially closed. Then, your flying squirrel has to knock the ball about to get the food out. It is also useful if you're going away for the weekend, to stop the flying squirrel eating 3 days worth of food at once, but also to stop them getting bored and destructive.

Wheel

Your flying squirrel will need an exercise wheel to burn off any excess energy and to keep fit. You need to make sure that the wheel has a solid floor. Wire or bar wheels can make an animal feel trapped and frightened, they can also cause serious damage to the fragile leg bones. You should look for plastic or wooden wheels as these are not only safer, but are also often quieter, and as these creatures are nocturnal it can be better to have quieter toys. There are silent spinners available for African pygmy hedgehogs that are also suitable for flying squirrels. These are available in a range of sizes and are safe and quiet.

Snack roll toy

These are wooden or plastic tubes with holes in. You fill the tubes with food, hay and paper and your flying squirrel nudges and scrabbles the tube, rolling it about getting their food out. These are brilliant short-term 'automatic feeders'.

Swing

A lovely idea for your flying squirrel is to get them a swing.
They'll soon learn to play a game where they jump from the walls
onto the swing and then to the other side, like a trapeze artist!
Not only is this good mental stimulation for them, but it is also a
lot of fun to watch!

Cargo nets

Cargo nets serve a similar function to rope platforms and form a
lovely resting place that moves slightly with the movement of the
animal and can be incredibly comforting. Alternatively, you can
hang the cargo nets around the enclosure to climb up.

Fruit tree branches

Fruit tree branches are the safest branches to use and are
commercially available from lots of places online and can be
obtained quite cheaply.

Street ball, basket ball hoop

This is a fantastic toy that some flying squirrels learn to use- they
enjoy the dexterity involved in the game.

Bells, mirrors and chimes

Having bells, mirrors and chimes hanging around the enclosure
isn't just fun for you to look at, but it actually offers some really
important enrichment activities and offers your pet a way to
control their environment. They will often climb to where they
can reach the bells and ring them on purpose. If your flying

squirrel likes the look of itself in the mirror it can entertain itself for ages, showing off to its refection.

Hanging den

There are some really attractive hanging dens out there. The solid hanging dens that have a nice secure base and strong hanging points are fantastic for flying squirrels, as they provide the opportunity for some natural arboreal nesting behaviour.

The interactive treat game - teach and treat

This is a fantastic device and has amazing potential for boredom breaking and feeding over short-term absences.

b) Home made toys and how to make them

Toiler paper tubes are so much fun to make into toys for your flying squirrel and are free! One good way to make these into a toy is to put some of their favourite treats into the tube and fold and tape up the ends. Then you can watch your squirrel tear into the tube to get at their treats.

This is also a good tip if you are going to be away for a night or two. You can use tube hiders for all of the feed they'll need and fill some with tissue paper and other things so that they don't get bored and lonely while you're away. This also stops them eating three days worth of food in one go and then going hungry.

It's also a good idea to make toilet roll tubes into tunnels by taping them together. You can make whole mazes from tubes and this is a fun activity in itself. This sort of enrichment toy encourages natural foraging behaviour and is a lot of fun to do.

If you're keen on building toys out of cardboard, you can make old shoe boxes into toys too. A stack of shoe boxes with holes through to each other can be a real brain teaser, especially if you hide things in and amongst them and use some of the toilet tube techniques from above.

Dig Box

In the wild, your flying squirrel would forage for food in all sorts of places. One way to encourage this is to make a dig box.

What you need:
A deepish, waterproof container
Substrate
Treats
Seeds of edible plants

What you do:
An old washing up bowl is the ideal size and depth for a dig box. To avoid bringing in any unwanted parasites, insects or germs you should fill the container with something sterile; rehydrated coir is good. Then you just bury seeds and treats in it. Any seeds that don't get eaten may grow into interesting things for your flying squirrel to play with.

On this note, it is a good idea to have a few dig boxes made up, some with fast growing, edible weeds, such as dandelions, planted in them. This makes for good enrichment and is a great way to let them express natural behaviours.

Cotton spool hangings

Another great idea for homemade toys is to hang on to the insides of thread or cotton spools. If your flying squirrel can reach this toy from the ground or climb down onto it, it can be a really good way to develop balance.

What you need:
Rope or thick string
Cotton spools
Nuts and seeds
Cuttlefish or other tasty things to hang

What you do:
First, stuff the spools with nuts and seeds as they are, then you can thread thin rope through them and hang them from the ceiling of the enclosure. While you're threading the rope through, you can join several together and hang other things like cuttlefish or piñatas from them.

Piñatas

Piñatas are very easy to make and your flying squirrel will have such a good time frolicking round trying to get their goodies out. Just like children, flying squirrels love the challenge of piñatas.

What you need:
String
Treats
Gum tape
Paper

What you do:

Simply wrap treats in layers of paper, taping each layer with gum tape. Then, tie the piñata to the ceiling and let your flying squirrel clamber about on it and tear away at the paper.

Rope perch

Using strong rope, preferably untreated jute or sisal, you can make a fantastic rope perch. These are excellent for enclosure enrichment and you may find your flying squirrel builds a nest on theirs!

What you need:
Rope
Tape measure
Scissors

What you do:
You'll need to measure the distance between the sides you want to stretch the perch between. Then, add about 1m onto this length to make up for knots and cut three pieces this long. Then, at about 30cm from the ends you just plait and tie the rope into each other to 30cm from the other end. Then you tie the six ends to the bars and leave your flying squirrel to it!

Fruit tree branches:

While not technically toys, these are brilliant for flying squirrels to play with and climb on. Fruit tree branches are safe, as they are not toxic for your squirrel if they chew. Under no circumstances should you give pine branches of any type. Pine can be very poisonous. Pear, apple and cherry make the best play branches and can be obtained easily from people who are pruning their fruit trees. If you ask about on sites like GumTree, preloved or on gardening forums there are often people who will give you orchard pruning free of charge if you are wiling to collect.

Paper Bags

One simple hiding toy is the humble paper bag. They can scamper in and out of them, scrunch them up as bedding, hide their own food in them and all manner of other fun things.

Fruit and loofah kebabs

Wonderful treat toys are loofah and fruit skewers. You can buy these online or you can make them. They are very simple to make.

What you need:
Bamboo skewers
Untreated loofah
Dried fruit

What you do:
This is one of the simplest toys to make. If your dried fruit is too big you can cut it up, though you might as well leave it as it is. Cut the loofa into 2cm slices. Then just stick the bits on the skewers. You can hang these around the enclosure or wedge them into corners for your flying squirrel to hang off while they eat.

Hanging den

A hanging den is a wonderful addition to the habitat of the flying squirrel. They provide cosy hiding places and, though it may seem counter intuitive, this means you'll be more likely to see your flying squirrel out and about - animals who know they can hide when ever they like tend to get out and about more.

Chapter 7. Play and enrichment

What you need:
Fleece
Rope or string
Lobster clasps
Scissors
Needle and thread

What you do:
Sew yourself a bonding pouch, as in the instructions later in this section, but instead of sewing on the lobster clasps directly, sew two lengths of thin rope or thick string to the corners and tie the lobster clasps to the other ends.

Cardboard fort

What you need:
Boxes of different sizes
Scissors/craft knife
Gum tape
A non toxic marker pen

What you do:

You'll be using the largest box as a base. Close the bottom and tape it closed. Draw on any windows or doors and cut them out. These should be at different heights so that your flying squirrel can hop about inside and climb through. Close the lid and place the other boxes on top until you find a design you're happy with. Then mark where the different boxes go and cut holes for your flying squirrel to climb through. Tape your boxes together with the bottoms and tops of the smaller boxes open. Be warned though, your flying squirrel will love to chew anything chewable.

A brilliant game for flying squirrels is to be able to manipulate their surroundings. If you keep things that roll, such as the insides of tape rolls and old plant pots, these are wonderful things to play with. They can get inside the cylindrical things and play about with them.

Crackers

At Christmas, Thanksgiving or just for the heck of it, crackers are fun.

What you need:
Toilet roll tubes
Treats
Scissors
Tape measure
Paper
Gum tape

What you do:
Cut the paper to 10cm longer than the tubes and 2cm wider than the circumference of the tube. Lick a small piece of gum tape and stick the paper to the tube. Roll the tube in the paper, covering the

tube and then stick the paper in place. Twist the paper at one end of the tube, then put in the treats and twist the other end.

Bean bags

These are fantastic things for your flying squirrel. Bean bags can be microwaved in the winter to snuggle up to at night or cooled down in the fridge for the summer.

What you need:
Fleece fabric
Rice or beans (make sure these are safe foods)
Needle and thread (make sure the thread is natural and will break easily if your pet manages to dismantle the bag)

What you do:
Just fold rectangles of fabric into squares and sew up two and a half sides. Then, turn the pouch inside out. Now, you can fill them with rice or beans and sew up the last little bit. Now your bean bags are ready. Be careful not to over heat or cool the bean bags, 1min in the microwave is enough.

Sunflower head

This is so easy it needs no real explanation. Grow some sunflowers. Cut the heads off at the end of the summer. Feed them whole to your flying squirrel. It is better to use the giant varieties or the older types, as these are more likely to have good seeds.

Cake

Cake is a great treat for your flying squirrel and can be cut up and frozen for later use.

What you need:
Nuts and Seeds
Insects or insect larva
2 eggs
6oz whole wheat flour

What you do:
Whisk up the egg and flour until the mixture is consistent. Stir in
the nuts, seeds and grubs. Pour the mixture into a loaf tin or can
tin. Bake in a preheated oven at 160C for 30mins.

Bonding pouch

For bonding with your flying squirrel you will need a bonding
pouch. It is also useful for being close to your flying squirrel
when it's grown up. You can buy these online but they are
incredibly simple to make.

What you need:
Some fleece fabric (woven can be dangerous)
Scissors
A needle and thread (make sure the thread is natural and will
break easily if your pet manages to dismantle the bag)
2 large lobster clips
A tape measure

What you do:
Cut a rectangle of fabric of about 30cm by 40cm. Fold it in half
so that you have a 20cm by 30cm rectangle. Sew up the two short
edges so you have a pocket with a top opening. Last but not least,
sew the lobster clips onto the two top corners. Now, you can clip

your bonding pouch and flying squirrel to your collar, neckline or belt- whatever you're wearing.

c) Useful websites to buy toy materials

Fleece:
http://www.minervacrafts.com/
http://www.minervacrafts.com
www.fabric-online.co.uk/
www.picotextiles.com

Gum tape:
https://www.vikingtapes.co.uk
http://www.turnersartshop.co.uk
www.uline.com

3. Training your flying squirrel

Coming When Called

Give your flying squirrel its favourite treat while saying its name over and over again. Do this daily and hopefully your flying squirrel will come to you for a treat! Make sure that if your baby comes to you, you do reward it each and every time!

Biting

If you begin to neglect your flying squirrel, it may start "wilding up" like with any small animal. You need to continuously handle your flying squirrel to keep it friendly and easy to handle, otherwise they can become huffy or sulky.

If a flying squirrel feels upset, left out or abandoned at all, this can hurt their feelings. It may seem very silly but if your flying squirrel has hurt feeling then it may play up. This can cause biting. This sort of biting is very easy to rectify. Make a short angry sound that isn't too loud – you don't want to actually upset them – and then pick them up. Hold your flyer to you and make shooshing sounds to calm them. Then you need to remember to spend more time with them in the future.

Also, squirrels seem to be more frisky in the winter months and can become protective of their nest and stashes. Even though they live indoors, they still have their natural instincts telling them that it's cold and horrid out and they must salvage their nest and food at all costs. You need to nip this territorial behaviour in the bud. If they bite you when you go near their stash, take them out of the enclosure and remove ALL food. Then stroke them calmly and replace them into the enclosure. Then feed them through the bars. This will teach them that you are in charge and that you will make sure they have enough food.

Sometimes even a certain food can make them hyperactive, peanuts especially.

If it is winter time, clear out any food stashes your squirrel may be protecting. You can also teach them not to bite. Some recommend pinching or tapping them on the nose, but this seems cruel and unnecessary. With a lot of small animals it is important to work out what they want to achieve by the biting and do the opposite. One rabbit trainer in the UK uses the phrase "rabbits that bite don't get what they want" when teaching her human students to train rabbits. So, for example, if your flying squirrel has bitten you when you were going into the nest and you can see no good reason for this, you take them out of the enclosure and remove all of their bedding from their nest. If they have bitten you over a certain food, remove the food. Eventually the flying squirrel should learn that if it bites, it will get the opposite of what it wants.

Chapter 8. Breeding

The mating season for flying squirrels is during February and March. When the babies are born, the mother nurtures them in the nest until they're ready to go off. The males do not get involved. Gestation generally last 40 days, but can be 3 days either side.

Flying squirrels are notoriously hard to breed in captivity, as the males need to be scrotal at the same time as the female is in oestrus. Your best bet is to have a group of flying squirrels, one male to three females gives you a better chance of successfully breeding from your flying squirrels. Once they have paired up to breed you can separate the pair from the other flying squirrels or leave them together until the pregnant female takes herself off into a solitary nest box.

The babies are born naked and defenceless with little or no ability to connect with the outside world. Their eyes are closed, their hearing and sense of smell are very poor and their internal organs can be seen through the skin. The types of flying squirrel most commonly kept as pets in the west are born about 2.5inches including tail long and grow to about 10 inches including tail. They are so vulnerable at this early stage of their lives that if anything goes wrong, you need to be on hand round the clock. Until they are around 5 weeks of age they shouldn't really be handled unless you suspect something untoward. Between 7 and 11 weeks they perfect their gliding skills and bond with their person or people.

Given that all is well, the mother will need no assistance with the pregnancy or the birth. In the wild they will give birth alone, without the presence of other animals and do like to be left alone during this time. If you're very close with your flying squirrel, you being there will not stress her out and may even have a calming effect, though you should only intervene if anyone falls.

1. Are you prepared for breeding your squirrels?

There are so many things to consider when deciding whether or not to breed from your flying squirrel. There are lots of lovely things about babies and little cute things abound the place, and there is a bit of money in it if you're successful, but there can be real complications and problems if it goes wrong. All exotic breeders, both larger scale and hobby breeders, are in it for the love. The margins in breeding flying squirrels are not as big as you might think and you have to be completely dedicated and prepared for the worst. The problems with breeding flying squirrels range from financial to medical and emotional.

Not only are there the financial implications of extra mouths to feed but much more seriously, if something goes wrong you can be left with either a huge vet bill or an impossible choice. Mum will need more to eat when she's pregnant and feeding, and the babies will start to try new foods before they go off into the world. While you may have found it relatively difficult to find a breeder with available babies, you aren't guaranteed to find buyers for yours. Are you prepared to house any offspring if you can't find anyone else to take them?

As with any birth, there can be complications with potentially life threatening consequences. One UK breeder I spoke to recounted a horrific incident where she was woken in the night by a high pitched distress call from her flying squirrels' room. On going into the room she found her female panicking on the floor of the enclosure. In the nest box two babies had already been born, but the third had become lodged, and in her obvious upset the female had tried to move around to get more comfortable and fallen from the box. The breeder rushed the mother to the emergency vet, but the mother and 3 unborn babies didn't make it. The vet said that because of the large litter size, the mother couldn't cope with the extra stress on her body. This loss really affected the breeder and it took her a long time to allow any of her females back with their mates. The two babies that had already been born died, one at 6 days old and the other at 13 days old.

2. *Special dietary requirements*

Any pregnancy can cause health problems, most of which can be avoided with the correct diet. High quality nutrition during pregnancy and nursing is vital. Continue to feed the normal diet, but you need to increase the amount of nuts, seeds, dried insects and figs to allow for the extra stress and nutrition drain. Nuts reduce the risk of gestational diabetes. Seeds are high in protein, which is good for building new tissues. Insects and figs will replace the calcium and other minerals to strengthen the bones, which is a major concern with flying squirrels. To avoid anaemia you should also up the greens, as iron is very important during pregnancy.

3. Specific housing

If you plan to breed, then the best type of enclosure to use is a 2 or 3 level one with a separable tower, such as the 'ferret and chinchilla high-rise'. This can be split into sections easily and has nice big doors for access in case of emergency. This type of enclosure also makes reintroduction to the group easier. You should give breeding pairs 2 or more nest boxes, one higher and one lower. This does a few useful things - it allows the pair to nest together as they would in the wild but to separate when they need to. It also means that you can tell when the babies are nearly here. In the few days before the birth, the mother will retreat into her own, lower nest box, spending more and more time hiding away and making the nest more comfortable. When this happens, you can separate the parents so that the male cannot kill any babies.

The male can then be put with the rest of the colony. After the babies have been weaned or are off with their new family, the mother will need to go back with the group. This must be done very carefully. The procedure is to have them in enclosures that are touching (side by side or on top of each other) for 2 weeks to let everyone get used to each other's smells.

4. Possible complications

If the babies come earlier than the mother or you are expecting and the male is still present in the nest or enclosure, then the male could kill and eat one or more of the babies. The pregnancy itself could put more pressure on the mother than she may be able to cope with.

Any breach births could slow the progress of the birth, possibly causing the miscarriage of any later babies and or the death of the breached baby and or the mother.

When pregnant, the mother will be more susceptible to infection and illness and must be monitored to make sure that she is putting on weight properly and that she doesn't become listless or sluggish in any way.

Pregnancy can also cause anaemia, as the extra use of the resources within the body can put strain on the blood. This means that keeping up the iron levels in your flying mummy is more important than ever. Kale and Swiss chard are a real boon at this time, because not only are they tasty, but they're high in iron.

As with any mammals, a foetus in its early stages can lodge in the fallopian tubes causing ectopic pregnancy, which is barely detectable in flying squirrels and is almost always fatal.

Undiagnosed thyroid problems can cause low birth weight or even heart failure in the foetus. This is very difficult to predict in flying squirrels as they tend to be a little jumpy at the best of times.

Fibroids can cause breech birth, preterm bi`rth or even miscarriage. Once again, this is very difficult to diagnose, as it can have no outward symptoms until the difficulties arise.

Gestational diabetes, while rare, can be a problem and doesn't usually have any symptoms in flying squirrels, though if your flying squirrel does become excessively thirsty you might want to take her to the vet to check.

If your flying squirrel mum is eating and behaving normally then everything is probably fine, though, as they are essentially wild animals, they tend not to advertise any potential problems.

5. Looking after mum and babies

Once your babies are born it is very important to have the right conditions. The temperature should be between 17 and 21 degrees so that the babies don't get too cold or too hot. The mother will regulate the temperature inside the nest, but it's best to do what you can to make her life easier.

Any bedding provided should be baby toe safe, so torn up tissue or fleece fabric. No woven fabric, as this can cause all manner of problems. Woven fabrics can fray and the threads can become entangled around little toes and fingers cutting off blood flow and causing necrosis of these extremities. Worse than this, the threads could strangle your flying squirrel or her babies.

Most importantly, mum needs quiet and dark and lots of fresh fruit, seeds and nuts. It isn't advised to feed live food with babies in the nest, but if you've got dried or frozen then mum will be wanting lots. Because of the propensity to calcium deficiency in flying squirrels you should increase the about of calcium available to pregnant and nursing mothers. There are lots of good calcium powders available to make this easier. Calcium powder on orange slices is extra good.

6. What to do if the mother rejects the babies

If you are planning to breed your flying squirrel, you need to be prepared for the mother rejecting the babies, or worse, dying in childbirth. In the event of either of these two unthinkable scenarios, you will need to hand rear the babies. If you are not very confident in doing this, you will find loads of advice and help available on forums. Also, youtube, once again, has videos of successfully hand reared baby flying squirrels such as this one, who is currently doing quite well.

http://www.youtube.com/watch?feature=endscreen&v=Eex4dX4r fAs&NR=1

You'll need a few things. It is best to have these in before the babies are born just in case.

Some sort of heat source
Fleece fabric
1ml, 2ml and 5ml syringes
Goat milk based puppy or kitten formula or soy based baby formula
Taurine
Colase or some sort of anti-bloat
Pancreazime or something similar
Colostrum (available from body building shops, also, ebay)
Cotton wool buds

First of all, your baby will need keeping warm. Under the age of 5 weeks, flying squirrel babies have real trouble regulating their own temperature, as they're bald and their skin is so thin as to be almost transparent. You'll need a heat mat with a variable temperature or an indoor electric propagator with adjustable temperature is perfect. Fold up a towel to about an inch thick and put it on top of the heat source, with the power on as low as it will go and put a box on the towel. Then put your baby in a bonding pouch or fleece blanket. It is important that the baby doesn't get too hot.

Once your baby is warm you can look to feeding it. Under no circumstances should you feed anything until the baby is warm and has been warm for an hour or so, as this could slow digestion to the point of drowning or the shock of a feed when the baby's metabolism isn't ready could kill the baby on it's own. In baby squirrels under 3 weeks old, start with a 1ml syringe.

In all honesty, babies of 3 weeks or under are very unlikely to survive, with the likelihood of making it to 8 weeks being only 25-30% but as a breeder they will be your responsibility and just leaving them to die is not only heartless but it is a crime. You need to be aware that babies this young may seem to be thriving and then suddenly take a turn for the worst. While this is harrowing, it an also be extremely rewarding if even one of the litter survive, though you'll probably not be able to make yourself sell the baby on!

As the babies get older you'll have a much better chance of success. If the babies are with their mother until they are 3 weeks old, there is a 45% chance of survival. As with all orphaned mammals and especially rodents, it is much easier to raise them to adulthood when they've some fur, and from 5 weeks onward you have a 70-80% chance of raising your lovely little flying squirrel to the 8 weeks they need to start to become independent.

Hand-feeding is the only way to keep the babies alive when they are so young. Choosing your milk is just as important as getting the right technique for nursing. Do not use cows milk. There was a breeder not so long ago on the Internet and in various forums pushing the idea that you could use 'scalded' cows milk to feed baby flying squirrels. This advice is very irresponsible and is refuted by any number of experts and people who have been convinced to try this dangerous method, only to have their babies die on them despite their best efforts. This woman, though she may have had the best intentions in the world and may only have been trying to help advise in a tight situation, has since been discredited, banned from the forums and struck off the professional bodies she was a member of. Cow's milk is too high in lactose sugars, which damage the digestive system and too low in protein and fat. The fats that are present in cow's milk are too large for most small animals to digest. The idea that heat can change the nature of the sugars and fats present in cows milk is frankly laughable and based on no scientific or empirical evidence.

If the mother dies in labour or the babies are abandoned very early, they need the colostrums that their mother would have given them in her first milk (in the first 3 days) to build their immune system. You can buy goats milk colostrums from the Internet and health food shops. You will only need a few mls so don't buy litres of the stuff unless you plan to breed a lot. Colostrum does freeze very well, and so you don't have to waste any.

Good quality, goat's milk based, puppy milk replacer are excellent for baby flying squirrels and these contain all of the nutrients needed for healthy growth, as the composition of these replacers closely resemble the components of a flying squirrel's mother's milk. A list of places you can buy these formulas is at the end of this chapter. Some Vet offices keep a supply on hand.

The mixing ratio is 3 to 1; 1 part formula powder to 3 parts water. Formula is only useful for 72 hours after it is mixed, then the vitamin and minerals will begin to evaporate and the milk will begin to sour, so mix small amounts accordingly. The Goat Milk Esbilac is made from a goat milk base, and does not bloat, constipate or cause diarrhoea.

If you're using a kitten milk replacer the best is powdered Nurturall Kitten Powder. Use 1 part of powdered Nurturall Kitten Powder to 4 parts warm water and a few drops of FeloviteII/Taurine the first day. From then on, use 1 part powder to 3 parts water for the next week or three for a richer mixture.

There are some excellent soy based infant formulas available. SMA is ideal. Using the scoop provided you should mix this formula 1 part powder to 4 parts water.

If your babies have lost a lot of weight or condition, you will need to give them a higher concentration of nutrition. If this is the case, feed this stronger mixture for only 1 week. Mix 1 part of the chosen powdered formula with 3 parts goats' milk.

You can adjust the strength of the formula based on your babies needs. You can tell if it is too strong or too week by inspecting the poo – lovely eh? The stools should be the texture of double cream and a yellowy colour. If it is thin you need to add more powder to your mixture, if it is thicker then you need to use less powder. This way you know that your baby is getting enough water and enough nourishment.

Make sure the babies are warm before feeding, and that the milk is also warm, but not hot. It is important to feed young squirrels slowly and the right way up. Never feed them on their back. Just squeeze out a little of the formula at a time. Wait for everything to be swallowed before pushing out any more. Once the baby has had enough, stop. If they start to wriggle or get uncomfortable, stop. If they've taken much more than they usually do, stop. Over feeding is worse than underfeeding. If you over feed, this could cause an aspiration pneumonia. Be sure to wake them up before you feed them. Feed them every 2-4 hours. Don't give too much at a time.

Chapter 8. Breeding

When you finish a feeding, gently massage their genitals with a warm, wet wad of cotton to make them go. Toileting is very important as the baby can't do this by themselves and they can die of ruptured bowels if they are not relieved. Sometimes, because the infant has not had liquids for several hours, and has not been stimulated (by its mother), it takes quite a long time to stimulate it to pee and poop, just continue to stimulate it after each feeding. You can immerse its bottom into warm water to help get it started if you continue to have a problem.

If the babies bloat with air, a drop of veterinary surfactant such as dioctyl sodium sulfosuccinate, "Colase" or, if you can't get hold of this, then a Gerber's anti-infant bloat will help them pass the gas. Also helpful are Pancreazime, a mixture of digestive enzymes and vitamin E. Crush and mix a tiny pinch with 10ml of formula. If the bloated abdomen is firm, they may be dehydrated and need more fluids, more diluted formula and a drop or two of cat laxative. (This is one situation where cat medicine is advised).

Chapter 9. Flying Squirrels, the law and insurance

1. What licences do you need in your country?

UK
You currently do not need a licence to own or breed flying squirrels in the UK. To import you will need a licence. Import licences must be issued in advance. Your pet will then be detained, at your expense, in a quarantine centre. Your pet will need to be vaccinated against rabies and be fit for travel. For detailed and up to date information go to https://www.gov.uk/pet-travel-information-for-pet-owners.

USA
As flying squirrels are native to the United States, there is no need to worry about import rules, unless you're going for one of the Japanese, Asian, Chinese, Thai, Pakistani or Russian varieties. As the flying squirrels available in the USA make such good pets, there is little point in looking elsewhere. Some types of Southern flying squirrel are protected and so you may need licences to keep captive bred flying squirrels. It is illegal to trap the protected species.
In Ohio you do need a permit to keep flying squirrels, you'll need an ODNR as they are classed as wild animals. If you are not sure, then you can always check your local state law, though if you buy your flying squirrel from a local breeder, they will be able to advise you on the specific laws and regulations that apply to you.

2. *What are your legal responsibilities?*

UK

Under UK law you are responsible for the health and well being of your animal. You are responsible for the nutritional needs of your animal.

It is an offence not to provide adequate food and water.

It is an offence not to provide access to shelter.

It is an offence to allow your animal to live in unclean conditions.

It is an offence to go away without making provisions for the care of an animal.

It is an offence to intentionally harm an animal or to knowingly allow an animal to come to harm.

It is an offence not to provide adequate veterinary care.

If you are having financial difficulties this is no excuse, but the RSPCA and PDSA may be able to help out.

USA

According to the animal welfare act of 1996, owners have legal responsibilities to their animals.

It is an offence to allow an animal to remain in pain.

It is an offence to deny, purposefully or by omit ion, access to adequate food and water.

It is an offence to cause pain or distress or allow pain or distress to be caused.

You must comply with humane end points. (Humane end points are chosen to minimize or terminate the pain or distress of the experimental animals via euthanasia rather than waiting for their deaths as the endpoint.)

95

3. Should you insure your pets?

The simple answer here is yes. You definitely should have your pet insured unless you have instant access to a few grand that you could spare on medical bills, should your squirrel become ill or have an accident. There are lots of places that insure specifically exotics and they tend to be cheaper and more comprehensive than ordinary pet insurance companies. More specific insurance will cover more of the illnesses and problems that are likely in flying squirrels. If you do your homework, you can find good cover for not too much money, though you are looking at about $300 or £180. Veterinary insurance could be the difference between life and death for your flying squirrel if you don't have access to a massive pot of emergency cash. Some owners like to put away the money they would spend in insurance for a year or so before they buy their pet and continue to do so once they have it, so that if the animal is healthy for its entire lifetime, they end up with the money at the end of it, but if your flying squirrel gets a serious illness or accident early on in life, it can be hard to find the money for veterinary treatments.

Chapter 10. Buying your squirrel

1. Where to get flying squirrels

So you've decided to get a flying squirrel. You're prepared for their arrival and you've set up the enclosure and toys. You've read all about them and joined forums. The only question now, is where do you get one from? First thing's first - only get captive bred squirrels. Wild caught squirrels may have diseases or parasites you're unaware of. As well as this, wild caught animals can suffer unnecessary traumas, which may manifest as behavioural problems later in life.

Where ever you choose to buy your flying squirrel from, be it a pet shop, a professional breeder or a hobby breeder, you should be looking to pay about $150-$225 in the USA or £100-£200 in the UK. If you find one for much more or less than this you may be being ripped off, so ask on forums to see if other people have bought safely from that particular seller.

Very cheap flying quarrels may be of unreliable provenance. It is important to know exactly where your flying squirrel has come from, so that you can be sure it is disease and parasite free and isn't inbred. Though this isn't always going to be the case, as some hobby breeders are only looking to make back their expenditure.

Overpriced flying squirrels may be a con. Perhaps it is offered as a rare, import or a hand reared from birth specimen, as these can legitimately cost more, but it is very unusual that an importer wouldn't have a buyer set up before hand or that a breeder will give up a completely hand-reared baby, because the bond can be very strong.

Chapter 10. Buying your squirrel

Do not pay for a squirrel you have seen from a seller with no happy customers you can refer to. This is where joining forums comes into its own. Ask around before you choose exactly where your flying squirrel is coming from, because if it seems too good to be true then it probably is.

a) Pet shops

Pros of pet shops

If you find a good reputable pet shop, they'll use reliable breeders with large stock to reduce the risk of inbreeding. They usually have good, traceable blood lines. Another reason to choose to buy from pet shops is convenience. Pet shops will often be able to source you a flying squirrel exactly when you want or are ready for one. A lot of good pet shops will have a returns policy and insure against death within so many days of purchase. Pet stores that carry or can order in flying squirrels, should be able to source most of the things on your shopping list for your flying squirrel.

Cons

Bad pet shops, whilst the exception to the rule, can be cruel, unknowledgeable, profiteering, and downright neglectful. A bad pet shop could sell you a sick, inbred, or wild caught animal and you wouldn't be any the wiser until problems arose and then you may not even be able to do anything about it, as the shop could have polices against returns and refunds. Do not 'rescue' from bad looking pet shops. Some people buy sad looking flying squirrels from pet shops to 'rescue' them. While these people have their hearts in the right place, it is a real problem for the animals they sell. Because the pet shop will not loose out by mistreating their animals and will simply replace the pets that have been bought by well meaning people, there is no incentive for them to improve their practice. By 'rescuing' some animals you would be condemning many more to poor treatment and neglectful behaviour. The best way to help these animals is to contact your local animal charities. The animals that are bought from these places are unlikely to thrive and may die very soon after.

Even responsible pet shops who source their animals carefully and have good aftercare often don't have the staffing levels to be able to keep up with the large amounts of daily handling required to keep flying squirrels easy to handle and friendly.

b) Breeders

If you find yourself a good breeder, they will be able to help you out with so much. They will have a vested interest in the long-term health and well being of their little ones. A local breeder will be able to hook you up with a good, reliable and knowledgeable veterinary service. They'll know where you can get the favourite foods and cheap places to get the set up from. The aftercare available from a breeder is second to none. They will often be on hand for questions for years after the sale. If you yourself decide to breed from your pets, your own breeder will usually be there to offer advice, help and horror stories.

Professional breeders

Professional breeders are people who breed animals for a living. They tend to be incredibly dedicated and enthusiastic about the animals they breed and often have started out as owners, progressed into hobby breeding and come on from there into professional breeding. A professional breeder will be very knowledgeable about the requirements of the flying squirrel.

They will often have a few litters due throughout the year, so you can reserve a baby months in advance and get yourself properly sorted. As preparation is the key to happy, healthy pets, this is ideal.

Pet owner / hobby breeders

Pet owners who move on to breeding are usually incredibly dedicated and care a lot about their pets. They often only have a few litters in the lifetime of their pets, meaning that the quality of the animals is much higher and care that goes into the handling and long-term wellbeing of their animals tends to be exceptional.

2. Choosing your squirrel

What to look for?

What you are looking for in a flying squirrel can be very different from what other people are looking for, though you do need to make sure it is going to be healthy. You want to see healthy, energetic parents, free from parasites and creepy crawlies. The animal you choose should be bright and clean. Their eyes should be open and free from any discharge. The fur should be in good condition with no dandruff or bald patches. There should be no bones felt through the fur and fat. The claws should be strong but not too sharp or too blunt.

You should be able to handle the baby before you choose, so that you can tell the condition of the animal and get some sort of gauge on their personality. Though this is very useful, you cannot rely on first impressions. If they are frozen with fear this doesn't necessarily mean that they won't be easy to handle when they are used to you. If they struggle out of your hand and bounce around the room, this doesn't mean that they won't be affectionate and love to snuggle up to you when they're a little older and settled.

If you are offered an adult flying squirrel be very wary. The owner could have a genuine reason for getting rid of an adult pet, but it could be because the animal has become vicious or is no longer good for breeding. If this is the case, it may well not have been handled enough and you could end up with a flying squirrel that you cannot bond to. You need to have handled the animal from 14 weeks at the oldest, and even then it would have to have been handled on a regular basis.

3. Useful websites, where to find your flying squirrel

http://www.jandaexotics.com have southern flying squirrels at $150

http://www.hoobly.com are a classifieds website that usually have babies available from about $150-$250

http://modernpets.webs.com are based in Ohio and require you to read up properly before you buy, their prices are not available on the website, but they are recommended by members of the squirrel board forum.

In the UK you're more likely to find them for sale from places like forums. Most exotic forums will have flying squirrels for sale, but be wary of anyone trying to sell you flying squirrels that haven't been handled.

http://www.reptileforums.co.uk

http://www.petsandexotics.co.uk

http://www.thesquirrelboard.com

And http://crittery.co.uk has information on exotic rescues, though they don't tend to have many flying squirrels in.

Chapter 11. Biology

Flying squirrels have an incredible sense of smell. The nose is small and sensitive and the olfactory glands are located behind the actual nostrils in the bones at the top and front of the face. The flying squirrel can find truffles underground and other flying squirrels from miles away using their noses.

Big and beautiful, flying squirrel eyes are excellent at seeing in low light conditions. They are dichromatic, meaning they can distinguish between most colours, except red and green. Because red and green are tonally very similar they cannot tell them apart. Some owners have done 'experiments' and claim to have evidence that their flying squirrel can tell the difference. This is very unlikely. Flying squirrel eyes are very sensitive to damage. So sensitive to damage, infact, that they almost always close their eyes just before they land to protect them form any dirt, dust or flying debris. This is where the vibrissae or whiskers come in.

The vibrissae are specially adapted, sensitive hairs around the front of the flying squirrel's face. These splay out like a cats whiskers so that the flying squirrel can be aware of its surroundings when it lands, without having to risk hurting their eyes.

The ears of a flying squirrel are round and furry, with lots of fine hairs to keep out dirt and dust. They have very good hearing and communicate with each other by sound.

Flying squirrels, like all rodents, have 2 pairs of long front teeth that will continue to grow and need to be ground down. This is usually done when the animal chews. The teeth should be in line with each other so that they wear on each other. If they are not properly aligned, the teeth can cause a lot of pain.

The patagium is the flying membrane between the foreleg and hind leg that the flying squirrel uses to glide. These are controlled by finely tuned muscles that pull the patagium taught and out of the way for terrestrial movement.

The skeletal structure of the flying squirrel is really quite interesting. The brain case of the skull is hard and light and the orbits (that's eye sockets to you and me) are wide and side facing. At the base of the skull there is a large hole or foramen magnum. This is how the spinal column reaches the brain.
The other bones in the skeletal system are incredibly fine and delicate. They need to be in order to allow the flying squirrel to glide in the way that they do. They walk on the soles of their feet and have long toes to grip with.

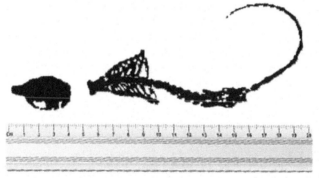

This shows the skull, ribcage, backbone and pelvis of a flying squirrel.

The alimentary system (that's everything that's involved in getting food ready to be absorbed into the body) is fairly simple as mammals go. They're well equipped to cope with tough cellulose. The oesophagus is lined with a mucus membrane, making the journey to the stomach very smooth. The enzymes in the flying squirrel's stomach need a warm, acidic environment to work best.

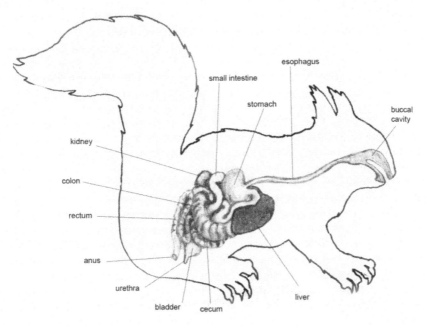

The flying squirrel uses scent glands high on the cheek, just below the eye socket, to mark their territory and to communicate with their companions. They rub themselves into each others faces and smell the mood of their friends.

The flying squirrel's reproductive system is very similar to that of most mammals. The females have a Y shaped reproductive tract

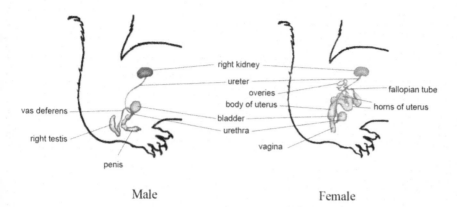

Male   Female

and 6 nipples. The male has internal testes and the penis is usually inside the body.

Chapter 12. Other important things

Don'ts list
A useful check list of things you definitely shouldn't do, so you can have a handy guide before you do anything new. This isn't completely comprehensive though, so if there's anything you're not sure about, ask on your forums.

Don't use homogenised squirrel pellets – this stops selective feeding.
Don't feed any cows milk products – these can cause serious digestive discomfort or even death.
Don't use medicines intended for cats or dogs – they are so much bigger that flying squirrels and are not rodents, their physiognomy is so different that their medicines can be very dangerous.
Don't allow any contact with wild squirrels – wild squirrels can carry parasites, fleas, mites, ticks lice and pathogens that have evolved specifically to affect flying squirrels and are far more dangerous than anything any of your other pets might be carrying.
Don't use woven or knitted fabrics – a stray fibre can choke your flying squirrel. A loose thread can become entangled around little fingers and toes, constricting blood flow, causing necrosis and limb death, or the throat, strangling the animal.
Don't over feed when hand-feeding – this can cause an aspiration and pneumonia or drowning.
Don't use water bowls – your pet can drown in very shallow water. Water that has become fouled can be toxic if imbibed.
Don't house in with other animals – no animals are completely consistent in their behaviour and it isn't worth the risk.
Don't use anything pine – pine is poisonous and flying squirrels

chew.

Don't leave males in with new babies – they may eat them.

Don't feed onions – onions are very toxic.

Don't allow unsupervised access to places that haven't been 'proofed'.

Don't use water bowls.

Don't syringe or bottle feed on their back.

Don't leave unsupervised with predatory pets (cats and dogs) - even if they get along really well a cat or dog could accidentally injure the flying squirrel and this could go untreated until you find out about it.

Don't leave your animal without food or water.

Don't feed any food that may be off – they are nonemetic (they cannot vomit).

Don't over handle a pregnant mother – if she becomes stressed she could miscarry, which is also a risk to her health.

Don't stop playing with your pet just because they've become huffy and grumpy – this will only compound the behavioural problems.

Don't use a galvanised cage - the process of galvanisation is to coat the metal in zinc, a heavy metal, which in high concentration can be poisonous.

Don't 'rescue' sad or ill flying squirrels from bad pet shops by buying them – this only encourages poor practice in these shops.

Don't feed them lettuce – lettuce is toxic.

Don't feed live ants – if they get out they make really bad housemates.

Don't use bleach or detergent to clean the enclosure or feeding equipment – even the tiniest amounts of this, if imbibed, can be fatal to anything so little.

Further information.

Information about flying squirrels as pets is becoming more and more widely available. It is advisable to join a forum for flying squirrel owners as they are usually owned and run by and for pet lovers.

http://www.flyingsquirrels.com
http://www.edible.com
http://www.transoniq.com
http://www.rattycorner.com
newworldexotics.com
http://www.thesquirrelboard.com
http://modernpets.webs.com
http://www.exotickeepersforum.co.uk

Index

CPSIA information can be obtained
at www.ICGtesting.com
Printed in the USA
BVOW03s1045291216

472037BV00007B/55/P